U.S. Special Forces

A Guide to America's Special Operations Units

The World's Most Elite Fighting Force

Samuel A. Southworth
Stephen Tanner

DA CAPO PRESS
A Member of the Perseus Books Group

Published by Da Capo Press
A Member of the Perseus Books Group
http://www.dacapopress.com

Copyright © 2002 by Da Capo Press

Cataloging-in-Publication data for this book is available from the
Library of Congress.

ISBN-10: 0-306-81165-0 ISBN-13: 978-0-306-81165-4

Da Capo Press books are available at special discounts for bulk pur-
chases in the U.S. by corporations, institutions, and other organizations. For more information, please contact the Special Markets
Department at the Perseus Books Group, 11 Cambridge Center,
Cambridge, MA 02142, or call (617) 252-5298.

First edition, first printing.

Printed and Bound in the United States of America.

Contents

Acronyms

AFSOC Air Force Special Operations Command
AO Area of Operations
APD Assault Personnel Destroyers
APFT Army Physical Fitness Test
BDU Battle Dress Uniform
BUD/S Basic Underwater Demolition/Swimmer
CSAR Combat Search and Rescue
DPV Desert Patrol Vehicle
DZ Drop Zone
FID Foreign Internal Defense
HALO High Altitude, Low Opening (parachute jumps)
HAHO High Altitude, High Opening (parachute jumps)
LAW Light Anti-Tank Weapon
LRRP Long Range Reconnaissance Patrols
METT-T Mission, Enemy, Terrain, Troops, and Time Available
MEU Marine Expeditionary Unit
MRE Meals Ready to Eat

NCDU Navy Combat Demolition Unit
ODA Operational Detachment Alpha
OSS Office of Strategic Services
PAST Physical Abilities and Stamina Test
PJ Pararescue Jumper
PM Paramilitary
RI Ranger Instructors
SAR Search and Rescue
SBS Special Boat Squadrons
SDV SEAL Delivery Vehicle
SEALs Sea-Air-Land
SFG Special Forces Group
SOAR Special Operations Air Regiment (Night Stalkers)
SOC Special Operations Capable
SOCOM Special Operations Command
SOF Special Operations Force
SOG Special Operations Group
UDT Underwater Demolition Team

Introduction

At this writing, in Afghanistan, U.S. Special Operations Forces are still on the hunt. Green Beret A-teams, along with Delta operators and CIA paramilitary warriors, have been scouring the valleys of the Hindu Kush, as well as Pakistan's supposedly impenetrable "tribal areas" to track down the core of international terrorists who perpetrated the atrocity of September 11. They are supported by U.S. Air Force SpecOps personnel as well as by the Night Stalkers, those Army aviation wizards who provide both mobility and fire support to our operators.

Earlier in the campaign, Army Rangers, U.S. Marines, 10th Mountain Division, and 101st Air Assault Division all fought in the theater when the heavy lifting was performed. The 82nd Airborne has recently arrived in the country, while from the start of the crisis the U.S. Coast Guard enhanced its presence along American shores and provided harbor security for the terrorist captives held in Cuba. After September 11, 2001, America's specialized elites went to war with a vengeance, and this time it was personal. As one smart-bomb loaded on a carrier deck was hand-labeled: "BEST WISHES FROM FDNY, NYPD + NYC."

Though Americans have always expressed a high appreciation for small-unit elites, the successful campaign in Afghanistan may have marked a watershed in U.S. military history. For the first time, Special Operations Forces were deployed not as the vanguard, but as the essential substance of an American war effort. These "quiet professionals" proved the worth of their training and the depth of their commitment by penetrating and dominating one of the harshest places on earth, halfway around the globe—and a warrior people that had defied the armies of other civilizations for 2,500 years. Special troops are no longer auxiliaries of conventional formations but can now (in tandem with the incredible reach of U.S. naval and air power) effect strategic decisions on their own.

This is a new way to go to war, and these American warriors are the best-trained and most deadly fighting force in the world. They are all volunteers (at least twice over) and they represent the best we have to offer when the bullets start flying. They are equipped with the latest and best weapons and gear that can be procured.

This book is an attempt to explain the heritage and current status of U.S. Special Operations Forces to the general reader, and to do so in a way that dispels myths and honors bravery. On the following pages we describe SOF victories and achievements, as well as setbacks and disasters. We examine their training and see how these brave volunteers have been pursuing skills and knowledge that have prepared them for the hellish landscape of Afghanistan, and to fight so well.

This book covers, in order of lineage, the units currently under Special Operations Command (SOCOM), and then the Marines, who have recently committed "a few dozen" of their legendary Force Recon troopers to SOCOM. Then we review other special operations-capable units from the Airborne to Coast Guard. Each unit consists of specially trained professionals, of the kind that America now calls upon for rapid deployment, special skills and combat courage in today's world.

As we appreciate the sacrifices of these warriors at a time of national need, we should also become familiar with their history, what they currently do and how they operate. We all enjoy the leisure and freedom to do as we please because these brave troops stand at the sharp end of the stick, out on the hazardous precipice guarding our rights, twenty-four hours a day, seven days a week. God bless them, and happy hunting.

CHAPTER 1

The History of American Special Operations Forces

As America enters the twenty-first century, its Special Operations Forces have gained vital new importance in the scheme of national defense. The United States now not only possesses the world's most powerful conventional forces but also the world's most versatile, highly trained, unconventional warriors. The attacks of September 11, 2001, demonstrated that foreign threats now assume an ever-wider variety of forms, from multinational cells of operatives to quasi-national parties to conventional regional powers. And Special Operations Forces make sure that America can rise to any global challenge—not just with overwhelming power but with speed and flexibility, daring and creativity. And let's not forget pure courage.

Nations in conflict have always needed all manner of soldiers, from the essential and overlooked mess orderlies and ribbon clerks, to the most highly motivated specialists. Within the

1

last two decades the United States has taken what were formerly ad hoc lash-ups—created during crises, disbanded just as rapidly—and forged them into the most premier elite fighting forces in the world. But these groups and this concept did not spring to life without a lengthy precedent, and an equally lengthy and sometimes hotly contested debate about their existence.

Americans have always had an affinity for unconventional warfare. This is largely because when colonists first arrived on these shores conventional battles in the New World did not exist. While Europe embarked on its period of "Cabinet Wars"—almost ritualistic competitions in linear tactics—the young colonies found their enemies to be the most skillful light infantry in the world: American Indians. The Indians practiced mobile, hit-and-run warfare, heavy on reconnaissance. Their few main-force actions always came as a surprise. They generally favored the raid and the ambush as tactics, as well as what we now call "snatch and grab."

The birth of special forces in America can be traced to 1676 during King Phillip's War, which is proportionately still the most devastating conflict in American history. King Phillip (or Metacomet, a Wampanoag Indian) had wiped out several colonial towns and his men had cowed the remaining settlers into hunkering down within forts. A Massachusetts captain named Benjamin Church devised a solution. After seeing a number of Puritan and Pilgrim punitive expeditions thrash through the forests and then fall into bloody ambushes, Church declared that the colonists needed Indians of their own. These were recruited from friendly natives and joined by European woodsmen—"Hawkeyes"—who soon duplicated King Phillip's tactics. Reconnaissance paved the way for devastating surprise attacks, and the colonists were able to regain control of New England.

By the following century the French had arrived in Canada

and, surprisingly, the soldiers of the effete "Sun King" proved remarkably adept in the wilderness. The French, unable to match the numbers of English colonists, were forced to employ Indian warriors as auxiliaries. This wedding of Indian tactics and ferocity with French leadership was a dangerous development for the English. The French and Indian War was fought mainly in the heavily wooded northeast. In 1756 a New Hampshire man, Robert Rogers, formed a battalion of woodsmen to "range" through the wilderness to intercept sudden thrusts by Indians and their rugged French advisers. Rogers' Rangers not only provided intelligence of enemy moves in the hinterland but also comprised a mobile strike force that could hit back at the enemy when least expected.

Robert Rogers is often considered the founding father of American Special Operations for his behind-the-lines exploits during the French and Indian War.

STANDING ORDERS FOR ROGER'S RANGERS

1. Don't forget nothing.
2. Have your musket clean as a whistle, hatchet scoured, sixty rounds powder and ball, and be ready to march at a minute's warning.
3. When you're on the march, act the way you would if you was sneaking up on a deer. See the enemy first.
4. Tell the truth about what you see and what you do. There is an army depending on us for correct information. You can lie all you please when you tell other folks about the Rangers, but don't never lie to a Ranger or officer.
5. Don't never take a chance you don't have to.
6. When we're on the march we march single file, far enough apart so one shot can't go through two men.
7. If we strike swamps, or soft ground, we spread out abreast, so it's hard to track us.
8. When we march, we keep moving till dark, so as to give the enemy the least possible chance at us.
9. When we camp, half the party stays awake while the other half sleeps.
10. If we take prisoners, we keep 'em separate till we have had time to examine them, so they can't cook up a story between 'em.
11. Don't ever march home the same way. Take a different route so you won't be ambushed.
12. No matter whether we travel in big parties or little ones, each party has to keep a scout 20 yards ahead, 20 yards on each flank, and 20 yards in the rear so the main body can't be surprised and wiped out.
13. Every night you'll be told where to meet if surrounded by a superior force.
14. Don't sit down to eat without posting sentries.
15. Don't sleep beyond dawn. Dawn's when the French and Indians attack.
16. Don't cross a river by a regular ford.
17. If somebody's trailing you, make a circle, come back onto your own tracks, and ambush the folks that aim to ambush you.
18. Don't stand up when the enemy's coming against you. Kneel down, lie down, hide behind a tree.
19. Let the enemy come till he's almost close enough to touch, then let him have it and jump out and finish him up with your hatchet.

--Major Robert Rogers 1759

Rogers is considered the seminal figure in U.S. special operations history, and indeed was the first to codify the principles of behind-the-lines warfare. His nineteen-point list of "Standing Orders" is still examined by professionals, from his timeless first rule, "Don't forget nothing," to his perhaps obsolete nineteenth: "Let the enemy come till he's almost close enough to touch, then let him have it and jump out and finish him up with your hatchet." In between he addressed march tactics, dispersion, evasion, how to treat prisoners, and other practicalities that still hold true.

But while Rogers' Rangers are properly revered in American history, it should be noted that they aggravated as well as pleased conventional force commanders. To some, the Rangers appeared as a band of rogues sans military discipline and "too fond of rum"; and the suspicion persisted that they created as much hostility among the Indians as they quelled. Rogers himself was later arrested by George Washington for corruption, went to England (where he was thrown in a debtors' prison), and returned to America to fight as a Tory in 1776.

When the American Revolution began, the British feared that the Americans would rely on Indian tactics. Washington won grudging respect from his opponents by insisting on fighting a conventional war along European lines, though he was ill-equipped to do so. The only bright spot during his disastrous campaign for New York came at Harlem Heights, when he dispatched Connecticut Rangers on one side and Virginia riflemen on the other to counterattack a force of British light infantry. The rest of the American army was astonished to see the Redcoats flee in panic for the first (and only) time in the campaign, though the Ranger commander, Thomas Knowlton, was killed.

While Washington struggled mightily to mold his army along strict European lines, Americans elsewhere fought according to their instincts. In the north, Ethan Allen's Green Mountain

Ethan Allen, the leader of the Green Mountain Boys during the American Revolution.

Boys kept the British off-balance with surprise attacks. In the south, Francis Marion, the "Swamp Fox," staged hit-and-run raids against superior British forces, denying them control of the Carolinas. The British dispatched a young cavalry officer named Banastre Tarleton—himself a raider of no small repute—to hunt down the Fox. The war took on a brutal, swirling aspect as Brits, Tories, and Patriots vied in small-unit actions between the occasional clashes of main forces. Neither Marion nor Tarleton were able to catch the other, and the British finally found the area untenable. The Revolution concluded as neatly as Washington had desired, when Cornwallis honorably surrendered his army to American and French regulars at Yorktown. But American skill at unconventional warfare had assisted the cause all along.

During the following decades, Americans on the rapidly expanding frontier gained unconventional combat experience in continuous battles against Indians. In Texas, ad hoc groups of

Rangers became the colonists' first line of defense against the fearsome Comanche tribe. By 1860 the Indians were no longer a threat in most of the United States but then the states decided to fight each other.

The Civil War unleashed the entire panoply of innate American military talent. At first, commanding generals on both sides kept Napoleon's picture in their wallets. Lincoln had inherited the official structure, if not substance, of a conventional military establishment, while the South's Jefferson Davis was a West Point graduate, whose firm belief was that only professionally trained officers should lead the Confederate forces.

This concept soon unraveled when the North invaded and occupied huge swathes of Southern territory. After Shiloh in April 1862, Davis signed an order commissioning "partisan"

Francis Marion, the "Swamp Fox," operated against the British in the Carolinas.

groups to operate behind Union lines. He rescinded this order two years later when too many of the partisans went out of control, plundering their countrymen as much as the enemy.

Still, there were disciplined officers on both sides who pursued unconventional, behind-the-lines warfare, coordinating objectives with their high commands. In the east, Mosby's Rangers operated in northern Virginia, preying on Union communications and tying up a disproportionate number of opposing troops. John S. Mosby's men lived among the population, and as partisans their guerrilla tactics not only enraged the Federals (especially one hot-blooded Union officer, George Custer) but

John S. Mosby stands hat-in-hand amid his officers. During the Civil War, Mosby's Rangers bedeviled Union armies in northern Virginia. (Library of Congress)

came under close scrutiny by the Confederate command. Near the start of his independent operations, in August 1863, Mosby's Rangers ravaged the supply lines of the advancing Union army, but they seemed a bit more attracted to capturing sutler's wagons than cutting rail lines. On receiving a report from Mosby through Jeb Stuart, Robert E. Lee commented, "I fear he exercises but little control over his men." Like many Rebel officers, Mosby was willing to suffer anything other than Lee's disapproval. His Rangers went on to play a vital behind-the-lines role in the struggles of the Army of Northern Virginia.

In the west it was a different story as the Federals—spearheaded by riverine forces—overran nearly all of Kentucky and Tennessee in the first year. In the wide spaces of the west, partisan warfare was disdained by both sides. But the Confederates found an answer to the North's gunboats in large-scale cavalry raids that counter penetrated the territory. Southern dash may best have been personified by John Hunt Morgan, who launched repeated raids to contest Union control of his native Kentucky. His destruction of Yankee communications and his bags of Union outpost troops may have been of secondary importance to his maintaining the morale of Southern-sympathizing Kentuckians. But in a demonstration of why regular army commanders tended to grow wary of special forces, Morgan went off the rails in June 1863 and decided on his own volition to raid the North. His twenty-four hundred men cut a blistering swathe across Indiana and Ohio but then were trapped against the Ohio River by Union cavalry and gunboats. The Federals put Morgan in a civil rather than a POW prison, to show what they thought of his tactics. A few months later, however, Morgan and his officers escaped, showing what they thought of the prison.

The key practitioner of unconventional warfare in the west, however, was a less romantic figure, Nathan Bedford Forrest. A

successful forty-year-old businessman from Memphis, he duti-
fully enlisted as a private in the Confederate service upon the
outbreak of war. The governor of Tennessee plucked him from
that position and requested that he organize his own company of
"Mounted Rangers." Barely literate and without military experience, he proved to be a military savant, waging war as though
from a blank slate of high instinct, inventing tactics as he went
along.

Though he joined main force operations as necessary,
Forrest's mark on the Civil War came from his unconventional
forays into Union-held territory. Typically these would consist of
two thousand cavalry covertly crossing Union patrolled rivers,
preceded by a spray of scouts. Once behind the lines the command would split up to assault a number of objectives simultaneously—ripping up rails, capturing Union forts, supply
columns, and herds, and retaking towns. Detachments would
make feints, and scouts would spread rumors to misdirect Union
response. After the raiders had swept the area, the force would
coordinate on a pre-planned schedule to make its way back, usually by fighting through a plethora of Union cavalry and infantry,
by then swarming into the area.

In late 1862, Confederate raiders achieved their greatest triumph—and a rarity in special operations history—by forcing the
strategic retreat of conventional armies. At the time, Union forces
were converging on Vicksburg. Grant was attacking overland
while Sherman was coming down the Mississippi. But
Confederate Earl Van Dorn's cavalry swept in to destroy Grant's
advance supply base while Forrest, operating farther north, was
demolishing Union rail communications in western Tennessee.
Grant abandoned the entire offensive, his seventy thousand men
turned back by the actions of some four thousand raiders.

In the summer of 1863, the Union tried to imitate Rebel raiding operations by launching two large cavalry probes of its own. Benjamin Grierson's twelve hundred men were able to ride from the Tennessee border through Mississippi to join other Union troops in Louisiana. Grierson's exploit thrilled the North, though it qualified as only half of a raid. The real trick for a raiding force is not just to penetrate enemy territory but to extricate itself once the hornets' nest has been stirred up. But then the Union didn't have much else to cheer about at the time. The other Federal raid, by eighteen hundred men commanded by Abel Strait, was aimed in a more dangerous direction, across Alabama to Georgia, but was chased down by Forrest and destroyed.

Behind-the-lines operations in the west eventually took place on such a large scale that unconventional warfare blurred with conventional strategy. Some historians view Forrest's cavalry as presaging panzer divisions more than special operations. But a look at the improvised nature of the Civil War raiders— starting small but with huge impact, fighting with more imagination than guns, more brains than numbers—reveals military creativity at its best. And as final proof that the raiders would qualify as modern Special Operations Forces, they were almost always underestimated by their own high commands.

After the Civil War, Confederate forces disbanded while professional soldiers from the North engaged the Plains Indians in a colorful form of guerrilla warfare. Reconnaissance and mobility were the requirements of this conflict and the army officially recognized the United States Scouts, whose emblem of crossed arrows still lives on in Special Forces.

The following decades saw only minor conflicts as America invented its military heritage on the go, as with Teddy Roosevelt's "Rough Riders" in the Spanish American War. During World War I, America mobilized on a grand scale to assist the British and French in Europe. Joining the slugging match under European rules, the United States contributed bodies rather than expertise, and lost 112,000 of them in six months.

In the twenty years separating Germany's aggressions, the technological revolution gained speed, and by the time the second round began, radio, radar, fast vehicles, armor, and, most strikingly, long-range air power had come into being. The new war quickly spread out on a gigantic geographic scale. World War II featured an imaginative proliferation of special operations, essentially laying down, through trial and error, the blueprints for everything that would come after.

On May 10, 1940, the German offensive against the Allies began not with heavy armor but with glider-borne commandos and paratroopers who seized or paralyzed opposing rear areas. The panzer divisions' path was paved by commandos. When the Nazis turned against the Soviet Union the following year, their conventional forces were preceded by Brandenburgers, special operations troops who seized bridges and infiltrated rear areas, often disguised in Russian uniforms.

The British, unlike the Americans, who had been in the habit of reinventing their military with each new war, had maintained a continuous establishment for centuries. They thus had a pool of trained officers perfectly willing to match the German tricks in kind. Soon an outfit called the Special Air Service came into being. This innocuous sounding name was meant to deceive German radio interceptors—it was really a commando unit. The SAS was followed by the Special Boat Service, who were amphibious commandos, and by the Long Range Desert Group, raiders who penetrated German lines with fantastic success in North Africa. Churchill had meanwhile decided to set Nazi-occupied Europe aflame, and the Special Operations Executive came into being. The SOE parachuted operatives into France and other countries to abet and direct partisan resistance.

When America came into the war a couple years later, U.S. officers were naturally interested in British expertise. In early 1942, Army Chief of Staff George Marshall met with Lord Louis Mountbatten, British head of Combined Operations, to get the skinny. At first the British desired the Americans to be junior participants in their own programs. But U.S. officials, from Roosevelt on down, insisted that the United States field its own special operations groups. The Americans did not want to be overly imitative so instead of calling their highly trained troops commandos, they recreated the Rangers. Instead of the SOE, they formed the Office of Strategic Services, the OSS. Once America was fully in the war, Frogmen, Marine Recon, and Air Commandos were born (with a mother named "necessity").

The 1st, 3rd and 4th Ranger Battalions—William O. Darby's men—were trained in SAS schools. But the 2nd and 5th Battalions were schooled at Camp Forrest, Tennessee. The United States had to wait nearly a year before its men could grapple with the Germans, but then the invasion of North Africa provided the opportunity. Darby's Rangers fought Vichy French, Italians, and then Germans, immediately achieving a high reputation. In every action, and during the invasion of Sicily which followed, the Rangers excelled with slashing, unexpected attacks.

With the invasion of Italy, Darby's Rangers fought magnificently at Salerno and in the Mignano Gap before Cassino. But then the Rangers were nearly annihilated in a German ambush at Anzio. The survivors joined the First Special Service Force—the Devil's Brigade—which picked up where the Rangers had left off. This unit also fought itself to death before being officially disbanded.

But for the invasion of France on D-day the Americans still had the 2nd and 5th Ranger Battalions on hand. The Normandy invasion provided the quintessential example of the value of specialized troops with the Ranger assault on Pointe du Hoc. This height overlooked Omaha Beach with 100-foot-high, sheer cliffs, and it was thought that a Nazi battery was in position there to sweep the beach. As an observation post or troop emplacement alone, the height was a menace. This was clearly a job for Rangers. At first light on D-day, the 2nd Battalion rappelled and grappled its way up the cliffs through a hail of German bullets and grenades. Reaching the top they held out against enemy counterattacks for two days, losing over half their number. On the beach, where the 5th Battalion was pinned down along with two infantry divisions under a torrent of German fire, Brigadier

Ranger reinforcements arrive at Pointe du Hoc on D-day. Hours earlier the attackers had rappelled up the cliff against Germans holding the crest. (U.S. Army)

General Dutch Cota coined a phrase by yelling, "Rangers, lead the way!"

Between the exploits of U.S. Airborne troops fighting countless skirmishes in the German rear, Navy Combat Demolition Units carving pathways through the beach obstacles, and the Rangers's actions, America's specialized troops proved invaluable to conventional forces in what was perhaps the most important battle in modern history.

In the Pacific theater, the 6th Ranger Battalion conducted missions behind Japanese lines in the Philippines, at one point liberating an entire POW camp, bringing out five hundred prisoners. The most famous special operations force to emerge from the Pacific War, however, was the 5307th Composite Unit (Provisional)—or as it was better known, Merrill's Marauders. Formed from three thousand volunteers, the unit was trained in India and then launched on a deep-penetration raid into Japanese-held Burma. Wreaking havoc behind enemy lines, the unit found that its only support came from U.S. Air Commandos—daring pilots who swooped in low to drop supplies or landed in jungle clearings to bring out the sick and wounded. Merrill's Marauders were so effective that the Allied brass could not bring itself to extract them, even when the raiders captured a Japanese airfield. Intended to fight through the jungle for three months, their mission lasted for half a year. Before and after photos tell the story of virile young men going in and walking skeletons coming out. The other part of the tale is that the Japanese abandoned Burma after their army had been shattered.

Back in Europe, the OSS had been flying teams of commandos into Nazi-held Europe, their typical vehicle being a black-painted B-24 bomber streaking across the continent in the dark beneath the German radar screen. These operators made contact with resistance movements, tying the partisans together with

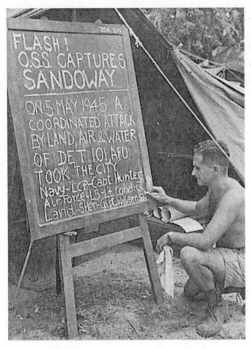

A member of Detachment 101 of the OSS chalks up news of the unit's latest exploit in World War II Burma.
(National Archives)

Allied resources and strategy. The phrase that described these courageous infiltrators was "force multipliers."

After Germany surrendered, all eyes turned to Japan which by that time was already reeling. In their island-hopping campaign, the U.S. Marines had developed select reconnaissance units, which paved the way for major assaults or simply took care of matters by themselves. The navy, too, had learned that its attacks needed to begin with specially trained advance teams to explore beaches or demolish obstacles in the way. In the Pacific War, Marine Force Recon, Navy Frogmen, Army Rangers,

A ship of Special Operations all-stars arriving Stateside from the China-Burma-India Theater at the end of World War II. Aboard are Merrill's Marauders, Air Commandos, Army Rangers, OSS troops, and Flying Tigers. (National Archives)

Marauders, and Air Commandos all established records of daring courage. Until the atomic bombs sent everyone home.

If, after previous wars, America had dismantled its military with amazing speed, the sound after World War II was like a vacuum as twelve million men were sucked back into civilian life. As Matthew Ridgway wrote, "The atomic bomb created for us a kind of psychological Maginot Line that helped us rationalize our national urge to get the boys home, the armies demobilized, the swords sheathed, and the soldiers, sailors and airmen out of uniform."

The Korean War thus came as a shock.

After World War II, all special forces, including the OSS, had been disbanded, with the single exception that the navy still held on to some Frogmen. The wheel had to be reinvented. But then Korea turned out to be a poor environment for special operations. After the first year the front began to congeal into a bloody face-off between powerful conventional forces. Hastily assembled Ranger companies were disbanded again. Though the U.S. launched White Tiger and other special operations in the North (just as the Communists tried to foment guerrilla operations in

The Rangers had a short but hot life during the Korean War. Here the 3rd Ranger Company prepares for a dawn patrol in 1951.
(National Archives)

the South), these had no strategic effect. In the end, the United States (or U.N. if you must) saved South Korea from Communist domination; but the war also resonated with the disturbing scent of a tie.

In 1952 the U.S. Army Special Forces was created, intended to operate in Europe in the event of a Soviet invasion. They were attached to Psychological Operations, a fellow descendant of the OSS. But no one has ever accused Dwight Eisenhower of being a SpecOps guy; and the concept of unconventional warfare languished as sort of a military backwater through the rest of the 1950s.

It wasn't until Eisenhower retired that special operations found a white knight in the form of the dashing young president, and former PT-boat commander, John F. Kennedy. The new president not only had an innate admiration for small-unit actions but an entirely different worldview than his predecessor. He considered all-out conventional war with the Soviets unlikely. Instead he foresaw "another type of war, new in its intensity, ancient in its origins—war by guerrillas, subversives, insurgents, assassins; war by ambush instead of by combat; by infiltration instead of aggression." He intended U.S. forces to be skilled in this kind of warfare. And he did not mince his words at a West Point commencement in 1962 when he said that it would require "a whole new kind of strategy, a wholly different kind of force, and therefore a new and wholly different kind of military training."

It is interesting to note that the three presidents under whom Special Operations Forces have most flourished—FDR, JFK, and George Bush (as Reagan's vice president and then president)— were all wealthy northeasterners who graduated from Yale or Harvard. (To them might be added Teddy Roosevelt and George W. Bush.) Under meat-and-potatoes guys like Truman, Nixon, and Ford, specialized elites were never encouraged. This is probably not a coincidence, and instead reflects the internal American argument over the very existence of institutionalized elites. America is, after all, a country that originally did not even want to form cavalry, smacking as it did of aristocracy. Within the American military establishment the creation of special, or elite, forces has historically met some resistance.

Nonetheless, Kennedy swept the entire country along with his admiration for elite fighting men, and with his assessment of future challenges. Investigating Army Special Forces, he found that they had been forbidden to wear their chosen headgear, which within the ranks had expressed their independent spirit. He made sure they could now be recognized as a unique force, thenceforth known as the Green Berets. In the navy, reconnaissance and demolition missions had been expanded to include commando operations and the Underwater Demolition Teams were renamed SEALs (Sea-Air-Land). In the new world of brushfire conflicts and guerrilla aggressions, there was a rush within the armed forces to form elite, hard-hitting, behind-the-lines capabilities. Special operations forces had touched a wave of public and political enthusiasm.

And then came Vietnam.

It all started well enough, especially with Green Beret detachments organizing the indigenous peoples in border areas to defend themselves. Other U.S. personnel trained the South Vietnamese army and air force. The British SAS had recently stopped a Communist insurgency in Malaysia and the idea was that U.S. Special Forces could do the same. But Vietnam turned out to be more than a brushfire, and America found itself fighting an enemy with direct arms pipelines to Red China and the Soviet Union, as well as a determined national military—North Vietnam's—that supported the insurgency with hundreds of

A Green Beret scans the landscape from a Special Forces/CIDG compound in South Vietnam.
(U.S. Army)

thousands of trained troops. America's conventional forces arrived in 1965 to take over the war.

As the conflict developed, Special Forces, Marine Force Recon, Navy SEALs, Air Force Commandos, and Army Rangers (who were actually resurrected during the conflict) earned reputations for amazing combat prowess. But it all turned sour as the United States was unable to force a decision. In fact, it turned ugly. The Green Berets, who had risen the fastest in public esteem, fell the hardest. Infantry officers who yearned for clear lines resented the "snake eaters" with their "private armies" in the jungle. Special Forces grew so fast that recruiting standards slipped and its operations became mixed with the even murkier agenda of the CIA. Green Berets were pulled from the conflict almost two years before the official withdrawal. And it wasn't just them. The recent revelations of former Senator Bob Kerrey provide a SEAL vignette. Kerrey won a Medal of Honor, but his true memories resided in a prior mission when his squad had wiped out a hamlet of civilians. After Vietnam, it took almost a decade for the United States to get the mud off its boots.

Vietnam cast the age-old conflict between conventional and Special Operations Forces into stark relief. The rule appeared to be that when U.S. conventional forces became fully engaged in a conflict, the space allowed for "elite" forces to excel narrows. During the Civil War, an army suffering fifteen thousand casualties at Murfreesboro cast a dim eye on the freewheeling cavalry. During World War II—in which 75 percent of casualties were caused by artillery—there was little sympathy for the notion that Rangers shouldn't be used in the line. In Vietnam, draftees in the 25th Infantry Division, performing recon of their own while combating NVA main force regiments, were not quite in awe of the special operations troops.

Combat experience trumps training. And when literally millions of U.S. citizens are engaged in a war, any preconceived idea of elites needs to be reproven on the battlefield. In Vietnam, specialized forces received too much ballyhoo going in, and thus endured more than their share of blame coming out of what turned out to be America's first retreat. If we had won, it might have been a different story. But after Communist tanks parked in front of the presidential palace in Saigon (now Ho Chi Minh City), and the conscript army returned to civilian life, America's military professionals stared at a very bleak landscape during the rest of the 1970s.

The United States had always demobilized after major wars,

but now it was done with a vengeance. Funding for Special Operations Forces, filtered through the services, shriveled by up to 90 percent. Army Special Forces, half of its groups already disbanded, feared for its existence. Fortunately, long-range thinkers devised a new role for the Green Berets that could bridge the period until America regained its self-esteem. The Special Forces undertook projects in backward areas of the country or Indian Reservations to build local infrastructure and instruct people how best to help themselves.

But Vietnam had left an echo that atrophied the rest of the armed forces. Recruitment in the now-volunteer army had shrunk drastically and many of America's best men resigned from the service. The economy was a mess thanks to an Arab oil embargo, and the only strategic imperative directed by politicians to the armed forces was "No more Vietnams!" The only military innovation was Delta Force, a counterterrorist arm of Special Forces, which was created because U.S. airliners were being hijacked at will.

It all came to a head in November 1979 when Muslim revolutionaries overthrew the Shah of Iran and seized the American embassy in Tehran. Disregarding every rule of international law, the radical government simply held U.S. diplomatic personnel as captives, daring America to respond. Iran bordered the Soviet Union, and a confusing factor occurred two months later when the Soviets invaded neighboring Afghanistan. Everyone was on edge and a conventional war against Iran—even if Americans had been up to it—might have crossed the threshold into World War III. Instead, Special Operations Forces were the answer.

In April 1980 the remaining professionals in the U.S. military tried to rescue the hostages. Navy helicopters flown by Marine pilots, joined by Air Force planes bearing Army Delta and Rangers, assembled in a secret airfield outside Tehran called

Desert One in Iran. Aside from incinerated aircraft and eight fatalities, U.S. forces left behind intact Sea Stallion helicopters containing secret files and equipment. (U.S. Army)

Desert One. It turned bad at the start because several helicopters malfunctioned en route, the rest were late, and the mission had to be aborted. Then it turned into a disaster when a remaining helicopter collided with a transport plane and a gigantic, self-inflicted fireball exploded over the desert. The next day, bemused Iranians strolled among the wreckage of American aircraft and abandoned helicopters, and then proudly lined up the charred bodies of eight U.S. servicemen for the benefit of the world press.

The national malaise had become national humiliation. The only silver lining in the Desert One tragedy was that the hostage rescue plan was more courageous than wise in the first place. In the center of Tehran, picture a Mogadishu writ large, but with U.S. forces having nowhere to retreat and no other help nearby. If the insertion couldn't be managed, let's not even consider the extraction with hostages from the middle of an enemy city of two million. But the failure of the insertion was bad enough, and from America's point of view things couldn't get much worse.

And they didn't.

Desert One kickstarted a new appreciation for Special Operations Forces among both the U.S. military and the public. First on the list was achieving long-range airmobile capacity. Two months after the disaster, a new unit was created, drawing on expert pilots from the 101st Airborne Division. This modern incarnation of the Air Commandos was called the 160th Special Operations Air Regiment (SOAR) and was equipped with the latest in helicopter and electronics technology. Today they're known as the Night Stalkers.

The Iranians released the U.S. hostages the minute Jimmy Carter left office; but the new executives, Ronald Reagan and George H. W. Bush, only increased U.S. Special Operations capability. With the Soviet Union bogged down in Afghanistan, the prospect of conventional war had receded. But Latin America was aflame with Communist insurgencies and the Islamic world was alive with new enemies.

October 1983 was a watershed in the history of Special Operations. Reagan had decided to apply American conventional forces—Marines supported by offshore naval guns—to quell a vipers' nest of warring factions in Beirut. But the Marine barracks was blown up by a truck bomb, killing 241 men. Another blast killed forty French paratroopers. Retaliation from the battleship *New Jersey* provided little consolation and Allied conventional forces were soon withdrawn.

In the Caribbean, meanwhile, the island of Grenada had fallen to Communist radicals supported by Cuba, and behind them, the Soviets. Expressing concern for U.S. civilians on the island (though in reality invoking the Monroe Doctrine), America invaded with Special Operations Forces. The island was secured by the second day in what looked to the rest of the world like an easy operation. But on the spot it resembled a fiasco. Four Navy SEALs drowned during an insertion. Helicopters couldn't find their targets and at one point three out of four crashed outside an undefended installation. Rangers made a chaotic low-level drop and navy carriers turned away army helicopters laden with wounded. It was for operations like Grenada that words like FUBAR were invented.

The last week of October 1983 thus confronted American political and military leaders with a serious, two-toned reality. First, conventional forces had proven unsuitable for operating in guerrilla and covert terrorist environments such as Beirut. Second, Special Operations Forces had shown grave inadequacies in Grenada. Following the tragedy at Desert One, specialized troops had been given priority and a lot of good men were now coming into the service. But command, control, and inter-service cooperation were still a problem. As always when it had to, the United States was energetically reinventing the wheel. But it looked like half a dozen wheels were being invented at once, running out of sync and in different directions.

Senator Barry Goldwater took the lead in rethinking U.S. military doctrine. The two-year study of his Senate Armed Services Committee was supplemented by Senators Sam Nunn and William Cohen, who focused on Special Operations Forces. Horsetrading their ideas with Congressman Dan Daniel, the resulting Nunn-Cohen amendment gave birth to an entirely new concept in U.S. military history. This was Special Operations Command, or SOCOM. It was as though Kennedy's vision of elite, small-unit warfare had indeed come into being—just a couple decades later than he had expected.

Activated on April 13, 1987, SOCOM tied together Special Operations Forces from the army, navy, and air force into a single unified command (see organizational charts, pages 275-277). Congress mandated SOCOM with the responsibility to prepare and maintain combat-ready special operations forces (SOF) to conduct special operations, including civil affairs and psychological operations. It is run by a four-star general (originally James J. Lindsay, today Charles Holland), equivalent in rank to his peers in the other services. Just as important, Nunn-Cohen placed Special Operations funding within the Department of Defense. This meant that Ranger funds, for example, would no longer have to be squeezed through the army budget but would came straight from the Pentagon as allocated by Congress. Special

General Charles Holland, current commander of U.S. Special Operations Command (SOCOM). (Dept. of Defense)

Operations Forces had effectively become a new branch of the U.S. military.

It wasn't long before this new concept of warfare was put to the test. In 1989, a drug-smuggling, gun-running dictator, Manuel Noriega, seized control of strategically vital Panama. Tensions grew until on December 15, Noriega's government declared a "state of war" with the United States. The next day a Marine lieutenant was gunned down at a Panamanian check-point and a navy officer was seized and beaten. Perhaps, in the White House, the final straw came with news that Noriega's thugs had also molested this officer's wife.

President Bush ordered Operation Just Cause and on the very next day SOCOM's resources sprang into action. Special Operations Forces comprised 4,500 of the 27,000 men that would invade Panama that weekend. And they were in the lead. Delta operators invaded a prison and shot up the guards to free a hostage while Ranger companies seized airfields, opening the way for the 82nd Airborne. SEALs knocked out Noriega's private ship and aircraft while Special Forces detachments secured cru-cial bridges and emplacements inland. Air Force Combat Control Teams coordinated strikes by gunships while Night Stalkers pro-vided mobility and firepower for the operators. In four days, the Panamanian army was beaten to the ground and Noriega had holed up in a church surrounded by U.S. troops. (He is currently serving a forty-year prison sentence in Georgia.)

The Panama invasion emphatically vindicated the SOCOM concept. SpecOps command coordination, communications, and weaponry was now seen to match the courage of its men. And the operation was significant for a different reason. For the first time since World War II, the United States had fought a conflict that had nothing to do with the Cold War. The Berlin Wall had fallen two months earlier and the Soviet Union was on the verge of disappearance. Ironically its demise did not produce "the end of history," as some had anticipated, but a proliferation of ethnic, national, and religious squabbles around the globe. If anything, the Cold War had paralyzed these ancient animosities while the world had lined up behind opposing superpowers under the threat of nuclear holocaust. Now that nightmare was out of the way.

In August 1990, Iraq's Saddam Hussein launched a blitzkrieg against his neighbor, Kuwait, with the good old-fashioned motive of greed. Iraq had the world's fourth largest army with thousands of tanks, artillery pieces, ballistic missiles, and a million battle-hardened men. Nevertheless, President Bush, cutting through a great deal of hand-wringing, calmly declared, "This invasion will not stand."

America's new and increasing emphasis on Special Operations Forces came to a screeching halt in 1990 as the conventional military stepped up to deal with Iraq. The army's General Norman Schwarzkopf hadn't liked special operators since Vietnam, and he planned to keep tight control of his show. That meant no cowboys.

SOCOM thus encountered a new challenge. Instead of running its own strategic missions it had to prove its tactical value to the U.S. heavy armored and mechanized infantry divisions upon whom the war against Iraq depended. Gradually they were allowed to demonstrate what they could do. Recon teams in the desert were soon tasked with Scud-hunting. SEALs pulled off dozens of missions in the Persian Gulf and along the coast. Night Stalkers and Air Force SpecOps penetrated Iraq in the air and on the ground. For the first time since Korea, Army Rangers fought alongside their old mentors, the British SAS.

But the most valuable SOCOM contribution came from Schwarzkopf's old friends from Vietnam, Army Special Forces (who no longer wished to be called the Green Berets). After President Bush had assembled the greatest international military coalition in world history, it dawned on everyone that they all spoke different languages and didn't have a clue about U.S. tactics, fire coordination, and combat air control. How to weld dozens of military establishments into a seamless whole? (Or in other words how to avoid thousands of casualties from "friendly fire"?) Special Forces A-teams spread out among the coalition forces, preparing them for what was to come. When the ground offensive began, the multilingual Special Forces advisers accompanied the allied contingents into combat. They became the knots that held the coalition together.

After the war even Schwarzkopf expressed appreciation for Special Operations Forces. And one effect of his 100-hour sledgehammer in Kuwait was to give U.S. conventional forces a decade of rest. Just as the Communists had learned in 1950, the petty dictators of the post-Cold War world had learned that America doesn't like blitzkriegs. As conflicts continued to flare around the globe, Special Operations Forces and U.S. rapid deployment troops resumed their place as first option.

Encouraged by the international cooperation in the Gulf War, and pursuing his concept of a peaceful new order, President Bush devoted American-led coalition forces to Somalia, where millions of people were starving under the chaotic rule of warlords. In 1993, U.S. Rangers and Delta Force operators conducted a mission in Mogadishu, resulting in a bloody battle. By then a new president, Bill Clinton, was in office, and he responded by withdrawing all U.S. forces from Somalia.

Clinton, who had evaded service during Vietnam, stayed consistent with his past by becoming the most reluctant president in modern history to commit troops to hostile environments. But as part of his mindset he was also the most reluctant president to cross swords with the services, which now included SOCOM. While the pax Americana declined to show its teeth during the 1990s (except with long-range missiles), Special Operations Forces continued to hone their skills, performing hundreds of training and liaison missions at home and abroad.

Shortly after George W. Bush became president in 2001, he was greeted by the most devastating attack in U.S. history. In the space of two hours on September 11, 2001, the World Trade Center in New York was destroyed, the Pentagon set aflame, and over three thousand citizens died on U.S. soil.

Fortunately America was able to respond immediately. While carrier task forces set sail and calls went out to the Airborne and 10th Mountain Divisions, Special Operations Forces were on the ground in Afghanistan within days. The full array of SOCOM's resources was deployed, coordinating resistance forces within the country, guiding America's vast long-range striking power, and performing direct action missions of their own. While Bush warned the American public of "a long, hard war," the Taliban regime in Afghanistan collapsed under fire in two months.

Today, while U.S. conventional forces maintain readiness to deal with any major opposing military establishment, Special Operations Command provides a mobile network of multi-faceted warriors, capable of difficult tasks and fast reactions anywhere in the world. Currently, SOF are organized and trained in nine principal mission areas, and based on their unique capabilities, SOF are frequently involved in a variety of collateral activities (see activity charts, page 32). Whether the threat be terrorism, guerrilla warfare or regional aggressions; whether action is called for in the mountains or in the desert, on the sea or in the air, in cities or in jungles, the units of SOCOM and their cousins among other elite U.S. forces stand ready.

Army Ranger Sniper

Principal Missions

- Counterproliferation (CP)
- Combating terrorism (CBT)
- Foreign internal defense (FID)
- Special reconnaissance (SR)
- Direct action (DA)
- Psychological operations (PSYOP)
- Civil affairs (CA)
- Unconventional warfare (UW)
- Information operations (IO)

Collateral Activities

- Coalition support
- Combat search and rescue (CSAR)
- Counterdrug (CD) activities
- Humanitarian demining (HD) activities
- Humanitarian assistance (HA)
- Security assistance (SA)
- Special activities

As mandated by Congress SOCOM has nine principal missions and seven collateral activities.

CHAPTER 2

U.S. Army Rangers

*H*ailing back to the earliest days of the New World, the Army Rangers possess the longest lineage of any Special Operations Force. They began as tough light infantry who could match American Indian war parties blow for blow on their home ground: the wilderness. To the main armies they added a mobile, quick-strike, and recon capability. Rangers were trusted to do whatever it took and go wherever needed to slam any "curveballs" the enemy could throw. And in the meantime they would inject more havoc—call 'em sliders and fastballs—than the enemy could handle. For two centuries the United States disbanded and then created Ranger units anew with each major war, even as the concept of Ranger warfare held steady in the American psyche. When the Civil War burst across the landscape in 1861, over four hundred militia units volunteered themselves as "Rangers." But only a few truly qualified. Another eighty years would pass before Americans would enter another confla-

One of the last shots of an Army Ranger wearing the traditional black beret. Controversially, in 2001 the U.S. Army allowed the black beret to be worn by soldiers throughout the service. In July 2002, the Rangers switched to tan. (AP)

gration under their own command and control. It would be the largest war in history, fought on a global scale—and the United States would contribute its own special expertise. As the ghost of Robert Rogers looked on, the Rangers were created again for the modern era.

History

On the 19th of June, 1942, a uniquely American unit formed up at a base in Carrickfergus, Ireland. The 29 officers and 488 enlisted men who stood on parade that day were the result of some high-level planning and far-sighted thinking in the early days of World War II. The conflicts in Europe and the Pacific had already featured the use of a number of special units as the war had opened up a pandora's box of unprecedented mobility.

Germany had unveiled its commandos in the opening days of the war as glider and parachute units attacked and conquered heavily defended positions in Norway, the Netherlands, and Belgium. In the East, the Japanese had used small-boat assaults and jungle penetrations to repeatedly outflank the British and drive them down the Malay peninsula. Not to be outdone by their enemies in creativity, the British had responded with several initiatives, including the Army Commandos, the Royal Marine Commandos, Special Operations Executive (SOE), the Special Boat Squadron (SBS), and the Special Air Service (SAS). These men (and some women in the case of SOE) were selected by a rigorous process that washed out many applicants, and then the survivors were put on a demanding course of training, always with the risk of being "returned to unit." The result was some of the toughest troops the world had ever seen. After December 7, 1941, U.S. Army Chief of Staff George Marshall crossed the pond to see what the British had come up with. He was impressed. And he also thought the Americans could make some contributions of their own.

Brigadier General Lucian K. Truscott Jr. was asked to raise a battalion of "super infantry" and in keeping with American military tradition he called them Rangers (declining to adopt the British term "commando"). In short order volunteers found themselves assigned to Achnacarry, the legendary Scottish training base where the British staged commando training. Truscott wished to set an American stamp on the new troops even while embracing the commando concept in many details. In these early days we can see the emergence of a standard for Special Operations Forces that has continued to this day: the arduous selection process; the dangerous and stressful training, including

General Lucian K. Truscott Jr., who in 1941 was ordered to form units of elite infantry along the lines of British commandos. Reaching back in American history, he decided to call them "Rangers." (U.S. Army)

live ammunition; the concepts of persistence, common sense, leadership, and teamwork; and the belief that more sweat in training equals less blood in combat. Men were formed into two-man teams, known as "buddies," or "me and my pal," and wherever one went, the other followed. If one man had difficulty getting over an obstacle, his partner was right there to help him. This was the beginning of a tradition whereby no man would be left behind, a concept originally articulated by the French Foreign Legion.

At the time there was debate over whether to use Ranger training as a sort of "graduate school" to augment basic training, then to have the men go back to their units to share their new-found skills. But by the time a suitable number of men had been found, it was agreed that they should enter combat as a unit as soon as possible. Full confrontational war on the continent was over two years away, but the Rangers could meanwhile engage the enemy. They could carry out some of the traditional missions of infantry, such as scouting and patrolling, as well as more ticklish jobs like raids, ambushes, cliff assaults, amphibious attacks, and night ops. Only men who had trained endlessly and were smart, audacious, disciplined, and tough would be able to operate against the great odds a small unit would face as the spearhead of attacks on Fortress Europe. They would be armed with lightweight but hard-hitting weapons, like the .45-caliber Thompson submachine gun, and would have to make up for their lack of heavier firepower (such as artillery) by being able to move faster and think quicker than the enemy.

Training included expert marksmanship with pistol, rifle, and machine gun, including night shooting and snap shots from awkward positions; armed and unarmed combat, including judo and knife throwing; mountaineering skills such as knots, rock climbing, hill walking, rappelling and cliff assault; seamanship and amphibious training in small boats during all weather and light conditions; explosives, such as bangalore torpedoes, a bomb on a stick used for blasting a path through barbed wire; map and compass work, including travel by night and with progressively heavier loads; patrolling and ambushing, including prisoner snatches to gain intelligence, and insertion and extraction drills to ensure that fairly large combat units could get in and out of extremely hostile places. The imagination and breadth of the training shows that while there was still some uncertainty as to how these troops would be used, the one sure bet was that they would need a staggering array of combat skills, and that they would have to exhibit the highest sense of dedication and purpose to accomplish extraordinary tasks.

The first American troops to face the Germans were a specially selected team of fifty Rangers who accompanied British commandos and Canadian infantry in a large raid on the French coastal town of Dieppe. While this August 1942 operation failed disastrously and the force was withdrawn leaving many casualties behind (including 75 percent of the Canadians), the Army Rangers acquitted themselves well alongside the commandos on the flanks. Their hard training had paid off.

In the fall of 1942 the U.S. Army mounted Operation Torch, the invasion of northwest Africa that signaled the start of large-scale Allied offensives to roll back the Germans. The first unit ashore was the 1st Ranger Battalion, seven companies strong, commanded by Major William O. Darby, the legendary Ranger leader. A runner near a field headquarters once tried to find Darby and was greeted with the assessment: "You'll never find him this far back." He was a hands-on officer who had the

respect and admiration of every man under his command. And, as has always been the case, such a leader was able

William O. Darby, the legendary World War II Ranger leader. Tragically, he was killed just hours before the German surrender in Italy. (U.S. Army)

to accomplish exceptional feats by combining good planning with a high level of esprit de corps. The Rangers in Africa performed a number of daring cut-and-thrust operations. They were experts at moving across rough and unmapped terrain, especially at night, striking the enemy hard before fading back into the stony wastelands. But they were still finding their way as an elite infantry unit, and in reconnaissance missions against the Afrika Korps learned not to make contact with the enemy if they didn't have the chance to break off and return with their vital scouting information.

In June 1943, two additional Ranger battalions were raised, the 3rd and the 4th, though Darby didn't exactly endear himself to other infantry officers by soliciting the best men from their units. The next month the Rangers spearheaded the invasion of Sicily, adding to their list of exploits. At first, Ranger units found themselves advancing without sufficient security, raising the risk of ambush. But it was the Italians and Germans who ran the greater risk with Ranger units in their rear. On one day, Darby's men brought in four thousand prisoners, a force more than twice their size.

With the invasion of Italy, as the Allies pushed the Germans back upon their land supply routes, the battles grew in magnitude. At Salerno, Darby's Rangers were thrown forward to seize mountain passes for an eventual breakout. But the invasion force was pinned down by vicious resistance and counterattacks. The lightly armed Rangers were forced to hold out for three weeks, depending on the navy for fire support. The Rangers were then committed to the Mignano Gap, where the Germans were determined to buy time for their engineers to fortify the Cassino line. Until mid-December 1943 the Rangers suffered 40 percent casualties grappling at close-quarters with the enemy atop freezing mountains.

The 3rd Battalion of Darby's Rangers embarking for the Anzio beachhead. Within days the unit would be annihilated in one of the most devastating ambushes of the war. (U.S. Army)

After a period to rest and refit in sunny Naples, the Rangers spearheaded the landings at Anzio. There was no opposition and it looked like the Allies had taken the Germans by surprise. But while the Allies failed to press their advantage the enemy hastily built an ad hoc perimeter, at first by pulling men off leave trains. Within a week the defense had turned into a hard shell. Just after midnight on January 30, the Rangers quietly moved out to seize the town of Cisterna, paving the way for an Allied breakout offensive. The 1st and 3rd Battalions crept through dry irrigation canals, seemingly undetected by the enemy. The 4th Battalion, with Darby, advanced by a different route and met immediate resistance. At daybreak, the 1st and 3rd realized they had been surrounded by German tanks, guns, and infantry. They tried to break through to Cisterna but the town was full of the waiting enemy. During the horrific five-hour battle that followed, Darby's 4th Battalion desperately tried to break through to its fellow Rangers but was stopped, losing 50 percent casualties. It was worse for the 1st and 3rd. German panzers rolled up and fired pointblank down the ditches. Rangers were pulled out and used as human shields for enemy infantry. In the end the battalions ceased to exist. Of 767 men in the 1st and 3rd Battalions who set off that day, only six returned. It was a devastating example of what fate could befall a lightly armed unit if unsupported by the main force.

The 2nd and 5th Ranger Battalions had meanwhile arrived in England to train for the invasion of France. On D-day in June 1944, the 2nd Ranger Battalion assaulted the Pointe du Hoc, a heavily defended cliff overlooking Omaha Beach. A menacing casemate on the cliff was thought to contain a battery of heavy artillery which, if left intact, could imperil the invasion by sweeping the beach with deadly shellfire. The plan was to use rocket-propelled projectiles to shoot climbing lines to the top of the cliff, but the lines had become soaked during the landing. It was only with great difficulty and under severe enemy fire from above that the 2nd Rangers finally forced their way to their objective. The guns, it turned out, had been moved a mile farther inland where probing Rangers found and destroyed them. The 2nd Battalion was counterattacked and held out for two days, losing nearly 200 of its 350 men.

Also present on Omaha that day were the "forgotten" Rangers, the 29th Battalion. Drawn mainly from the 29th Infantry Division, these men had graduated from the brutal training and went on to perform several missions in Norway and off the coast of France. But then the army dissolved the unit, dispersing the men back throughout the division. This was done according to the alternate theory, held by many officers, that Ranger training should be used to stiffen regular divisions, not create separate elites. (Some men were so disappointed they transferred to Airborne.) But as we now know, the 29th Infantry Division, a National Guard unit, was destined to be half of the first wave on D-day. It can't be measured how effective the 29th's Rangers were in that crucial battle. What we do know is that after being paralyzed at the waterline by murderous German fire, the Americans only began to advance when a few intrepid individuals up and down the beach suddenly began to lead breakouts. That morning Dutch Coda, assistant commander of the 29th Division, yelled, "Rangers, lead the way!" At the time he was standing amid men of the 5th Ranger Battalion which had drifted into his sector. But he might just as well have meant his own Rangers scattered throughout the 29th.

The 6th Ranger Battalion in the Pacific participated in a POW rescue at Cabanatuan that also illustrated their multiple strengths. Operating behind enemy lines as the Japanese retreated through the Philippines, Rangers made a stealthy approach to the POW camp, spent some time observing and planning, and then were able to hit the camp so hard that all the prisoners were rescued without injury and the Japanese forces were completely destroyed.

In January 1944, a regiment-sized raiding force penetrated Japanese lines in Burma. Popularly known as Merrill's Marauders after its commander, Frank D. Merrill, this Ranger-type unit operated in the jungle for six months, wreaking havoc on enemy rear areas. Officially, this unit was designated the 475th Regiment after completing its mission, and redesignated the 75th Regiment when it was reactivated in 1954.

At the end of World War II all the Ranger battalions that had not already been destroyed were disbanded, but the concept of

Rangers was reinvented for the Korean War. The first Ranger company sent into combat had the unlucky task of spearheading Eighth Army's "End the War" offensive toward the Yalu River in November 1950. American Intelligence didn't realize that a 300,000-man Chinese army was hiding in the hills. The company was destroyed on the first night of the Chinese counteroffensive. Twenty-one survivors, most of them wounded, made it back to the lines. Eventually six of fourteen Ranger companies were put into the field attached to various regular army units, fighting as scouts and behind-the-lines raiders. As the front solidified, however, they began to be used as regular infantry. Their supply was awkward in that Rangers drew food and ammunition from units to which they were attached, causing some clumsy situations. The doctrine of how commanders should use Rangers was also unclear. As "special" infantry they may just have been handed the worst tasks, for example taking a hill that had resisted all other efforts. In several genuine Ranger operations, airborne drops were employed for the first time, though in one case a squad was caught by the Chinese and nearly wiped out. By 1952 the Ranger units had been disbanded once again, though Ranger training continued, in the belief that the course should supply elite infantry to be spread throughout the army, which many officers had been recommending all along.

Ranger training was standardized during this time, but it was not until near the end of the Vietnam War that once again Ranger units would arise, from the various LRRP (Long Range Reconnaissance Patrols) that had been operating successfully in the jungles of southeast Asia. These "Lurps" would be given a certain area to patrol, and went into the field with only what they could carry, staying out on watch for up to six or seven days, avoiding contact if they could, and reporting back enemy movements. In their creative use of camouflage and stealthy move-

Rangers provide a demonstration of hand-to-hand combat for the benefit of South Vietnamese soldiers during the Vietnam War. (AP)

ment they were a welcome throwback to the original Rangers from the French and Indian War, undaunted by terrain, weather, the night, or the enemy.

In 1969 the LRRPs were designated Rangers and then organized as the 75th Regiment, the final unit designation of Merrill's Marauders. By 1974 they had been formed into Airborne Ranger battalions, with additional missions involving strategic national objectives. Their training came to include the securing of air bases, and it was in this role that Company C, 1st Battalion, 75th Rangers found themselves called to Egypt in April of 1980.

Their part of the aborted Iranian hostage rescue mission known as Eagle Claw was to secure an airfield thirty-five miles south of Tehran, with other Rangers standing ready to assist Delta Force in freeing the hostages. On that chaotic night the Rangers providing security at Desert One took into custody a bus load of Iranian civilians, and also destroyed a fuel truck that refused to stop. But malfunctioning helicopters and an aviation accident at Desert One meant that most of the Rangers never left their base in Egypt. Still, it was an indication of what could be done with the modern-day Rangers, and pointed the way for future operations.

By October 1983, when American students were taken hostage on the island of Grenada, the Rangers were up and ready to move within hours, and this despite incomplete intelligence about the defenders of the island, and outdated tourist maps. They were to parachute in and seize the airport at Point Salines, then secure the campus of True Blue where American students were being kept, and then attack a camp at Calivigny. But there were difficulties even getting to the island. Six hundred Rangers in ten C-130s were part of a large and quickly assembled plan that changed frequently right up until the moment they bailed out. Pilots became confused by bad weather, radios failed to work, and the pre-mission planning had to be jettisoned. Because of uncertainty about the state of the runway at Point Salines, Rangers first prepared to jump, then were told they would land in the C-130s with all of their heavier gear (such as small helicopters and recoilless rifles), and then were told they would definitely be using parachutes and have to wait for the rest of the gear. They were finally able to jump at dawn, a mere five hundred feet off the ground, but only forty men landed out of an initial force of two hundred; the other planes were forced to abort by heavy ground fire. The few men who did land called in AC-

130 Spectre gunships to open fire on the enemy who overlooked them. After clearing the runway of obstacles, the Rangers on the ground were joined by the rest of their unit. At this point they began to move toward their objectives and were able to free the students at the True Blue campus—but there they learned that more students were being held elsewhere. One Ranger was killed while trying to negotiate with Cuban troops to surrender. As they pushed further into the island, four Rangers were slain when they were caught in an enemy ambush.

An assault on a second campus was planned for the next day, but once again the Rangers were hindered by ineffective support and aerial confusion on their way to the target. Nevertheless, they were able to find and free the remaining students with help from Spectre gunships, and then fend off attacks by Cuban troops in armored personnel carriers. Almost nothing had gone according to plan in Grenada, but the Rangers were eventually able to accomplish their missions. A troubling note was introduced when U.S. Army Black Hawk helicopters with wounded Rangers aboard were refused permission to land on U.S. Navy aircraft carriers because the pilots hadn't received training to do so, and there was also an issue of the navy refusing to refuel army aircraft. It was clear that the Special Operations community wasn't all together on the same page, while conventional forces seemed to be reading a different book. But once again the Rangers had used their light infantry skills and initiative to complete daunting tasks, despite confusion and uncertainty, as well as numerous tactical and strategic mistakes.

The 1989 invasion of Panama to oust General Manuel Noriega was planned much better, and though a larger operation it came off more smoothly. Special Operations Command had been created in 1987, marking a watershed in the employment and coordination of America's specialized forces. And Rangers had been practicing missions for several years by the time they were ordered into Panama. The three Ranger objectives were Torillos International Airport, Rio Hata Military Airfield, and Noriega's private beach house. The jump at Rio Hata was again at a bare minimum five hundred feet, and under fire from the ground. Despite these daunting conditions, the airfield was secured in two hours and the 82nd Airborne came floating in. (Their first combat drop since World War II.) Following this success the Rangers were able, as part of the larger invasion force, to secure the country in a few days. Their fast deployment and sure-footed handling of tasks were a signal that U.S. Army Rangers were back up to speed after many years of neglect.

In 1991 during Desert Storm, small elements of Rangers performed a variety of tasks, including training Saudi troops, conducting raids, and destroying SCUD missiles. They also secured remote airfields and performed long-range scouting missions, during some of which they remained undetected for days some one hundred miles behind enemy lines despite proximity to hostile Iraqi troops.

It was in Somalia that the U.S. Airborne Rangers faced some of the fiercest fighting since Vietnam, establishing in the process a reputation for unsurpassed courage. The situation in Somalia was grim: six factions led by warlords fought for control of the benighted African country, stealing any and all relief materiel being provided by the United Nations. The U.S. military stepped in, not wearing the blue berets of U.N. peacekeepers, but using Special Operations Forces to deal with the warlords, restoring the supply of aid to the starving population. Muhammad Aidid was considered the worst of the criminal warlords. When a Somali agent indicated that there was to be a high-level meeting of Aidid's aides on October 3, 1993, a force of seventy-five Rangers and forty Delta troopers went into action.

47

President George W. Bush visiting Fort Bragg in March 2002. He witnessed a demonstration of Rangers transported by Night Stalker Chinooks. The Rangers disembarked from the helicopters riding motorcycles and SOF vehicles to take down a mock village.
(U.S. Army)

The plan was to fast-rope out of helicopters onto the building where the leaders were meeting. At the same time a vehicle convoy would drive to the site and take everyone back to the U.S. base outside Mogadishu. It was to be a daylight mission, rapidly executed, and thus the Rangers left behind their bayonets, canteens, and night-vision goggles. There was little room for error. When the code word "Irene" was sent out, fourteen helicopters lifted off to insert the Rangers and Delta teams—Delta to do the "snatching" and the Rangers to provide security—while the ground convoy left the American base. After twenty minutes the Somali leaders had been captured, and only one Ranger had been hurt, by falling to the ground while fast-roping. But soon after that things got substantially worse.

Their target was a mere three blocks from the Bakara Market, known as "The Black Sea," and the Somalis had been watching the American troops operate for months. They knew the drill. Seeing the helicopters overhead, crowds used these indicators to gather, and soon armed mobs were converging on the Ranger and Delta operators. In addition to the ubiquitous AK-47 automatic rifles, a previously unknown cache of RPGs (Soviet-made, rocket-propelled grenade launchers) were turned on the men and machines. Two Black Hawk helicopters were hit by RPGs and crashed, killing some and wounding the rest of their crews. In all, five helicopters were downed that day, though three managed to limp close to friendly lines before setting down. But the Rangers were now surrounded by hordes of Somalis and the mission had changed to protecting the surviving crews of the downed helicopters. The convoy sent to extract the Rangers and Delta soldiers meanwhile got lost in the narrow maze of streets. Bullets and rockets turned the vehicles into sieves as they made wrong turns, returning fire en route. The convoy finally had to return to base to drop off its wounded and reorient.

Back in the center of Mogadishu, the Rangers showed their ability to improvise on the fly and inflict staggering casualties on their enemies. The last of our troops didn't get to safety until the next morning, having spent the night fighting their way through neighborhoods bristling with hostile Somali gunmen. When the smoke cleared, eighteen American soldiers had lost their lives, two Ranger-qualified Delta troopers had been posthumously awarded the Medal of Honor, and the streets and rooftops of Mogadishu were strewn with hundreds of enemy dead.

Eight years later the Rangers were back in combat, parachuting into the desert south of Kandahar as part of a bold strike on a new enemy, the Taliban warriors and Al Qaeda terrorists of Afghanistan. By now the Rangers were performing a familiar task: securing airfields in daring night drops, providing muscle for Delta operators, and providing their hard-hitting and fast-moving skills, in any weather or terrain, against any kind of enemy.

Training

Getting to be a Ranger is among the more difficult tasks anyone can ask of themselves—and that's still the way you have to do it: volunteer. There was once a discussion at high levels about making Ranger training mandatory for all U.S. Army officers, but it was determined that this would undermine the pride that volunteers felt and lessen the effectiveness of these fine troops. The Ranger tab (a curved black patch bordered in gold with letters spelling out "RANGER") is among the most coveted, as well as low-key, of all patches, but when you see it you know the man wearing it has been trained to fight harder than all other troops, and to let nothing stand in his way. That's the way the RI's (Ranger Instructors) want it. And by all accounts, what the RI's want is what they get.

Top: *A sergeant from the 5th Ranger Training Battalion leads a patrol through one of the many conditions Rangers are expected to face.* (U.S. Army)

Bottom: *A Ranger participating in maneuvers at the Joint Readiness Training Center at Fort Polk, Louisiana.* (DVIC)

The World War II Rangers were trained by the British commandos in Scotland, but the first class to be awarded the modern Ranger tab graduated in 1952. After trying a number of different schedules and phases, in 1992 it was decided that Ranger training would consist of sixty-five days, moving from Fort Benning, Georgia, to Fort Bliss, Texas, back to Dahlonega, Georgia, and then to Eglin Air Force Base in Florida, with a different emphasis at each stop. Fort Benning provides the initial training where recruits are tested physically and mentally by long hours of exercise and close observation. Fort Bliss provides desert training similar to what would be encountered in the Middle East. Dahlonega is where mountain warfare and all of its attendant skills are taught, and Eglin is where future Rangers get their taste of jungle warfare.

Every phase is increasingly stressful, and this is augmented by the lack of food and sleep. Days begin early and finish late, and food is rationed to one MRE ("Meals Ready to Eat," also known as "Meals Rejected by Everyone") during some phases. On good nights, and before parachute jumps, students get four or five hours of sleep, although those are rare. The idea is not simply to torment students into failing or quitting (two-thirds of them will not pass), but to make sure that these soldiers can adapt and overcome anything. Even tough guys and show-offs are at their worst when cold, tired, and hungry, and it is then that guts and automatic response to training will pull them through.

Any male sergeant or officer in the U.S. Army or other services, in good shape and with recommendations, can enter Ranger training. They arrive with their medical and military records, but no rank or unit insignia. All will be equally tested. During this first period, the Ranger Assessment Phase, they are led through running, push-ups, sit-ups, and chin-ups, and are then required to pass a three part swim test. First, they need to swim about fifty feet in full combat gear, including boots. Then, they need to discard all of their gear and get out of the water. Next they have to walk off a plank about ten feet off the water in full combat gear, and do all of this without panic. Anyone who has ever tried to swim while clothed will realize it takes a cool head to pull this off. The goal in the running is to maintain a pace of a mile every eight minutes or faster, and to be able to run five miles in forty minutes, which is a good clip. There are also land navigation, both day and night, and endless push-ups and flutter kicks to keep everyone from getting bored.

The "Ranger Stakes" were instituted to make sure that everyone, even if they are not regular U.S. Army, is on the same page with basic weapons, and this eliminates time-consuming training for foreign troops and members of other services. The eleven events, all of which must be executed smartly, begin with the care, cleaning, loading, and ranging of the M-60 machine gun, the standard man-carried heavy weapon of a platoon. Then it moves to the setting up and detonation of the M181A1 Claymore, which is a rectangle of explosives with embedded steel balls, designed to cover a wide area such as an ambush site or used for perimeter security while a team rests. The dangerous side of this munition is helpfully marked "Towards Enemy." Then the students are asked to use basic communications gear and coding procedures, and then on to the M-16 rifle, the basic 5.56mm-long arm of the U.S. military. The early models of this rifle became notorious for jamming in combat in Vietnam, and while they have been improved, it is as important now as it has always been to keep the rifle clean and ready to operate at all times. The next drill is the use of grenades, which can be tricky because they explode in all directions, and then the cleaning and use of the M203 grenade launcher.

There are also increasingly lengthy and challenging obstacle courses, including narrow walkways thirty feet in the air over mud pits, and ten foot walls to be overcome, and wires down which to slide into water. Hand-to-hand combat for the Rangers doesn't mean having a complex series of moves to remember or a lot of fancy footwork; any method that works to disable an opponent is encouraged, and that includes striking with any part of the body, and from any position. Also included are helicopter jumps and patrols in which leadership is stressed.

On Day 16 it's off to Fort Bliss, Texas, where the intricacies of desert combat and survival are taught. There is food and water in the desert, but it takes focus and confidence to find it. The pace of skills and the complexity also increases here, as the would-be Rangers begin to explore the tasks at which they will be expected to excel in more depth, such as patrolling, reconnaissance, ambushes, raids, reaction to being ambushed, searching bodies for booby traps and documents, clearing trenches, crossing barbed wire, and assaulting bunkers. Each student is given a chance to lead, and their leadership strengths and weaknesses are closely noted by their instructors. One basic template is METT-T, which stands for Mission, Enemy, Terrain, Troops, and Time Available. Failure to take any of these into account will result in a negative assessment. There are also such subtle points as weather and morale, both of which can spell the success or failure of a mission. Interestingly, if a patrol fails due to weather, they will still get a passing grade if they tried as hard as they could despite whatever the skies had to throw in their way.

On Day 33, the by-now exhausted students go to Camp Merrill (named for the commander of Merrill's Marauders) in Dahlonega, Georgia, to start the mountain phase of their training. Here they will begin by learning climbing knots, use of rappelling and climbing gear such as the Figure Eight belay and descent device; how to manage and use rope carefully so it is not abraded by sharp rocks or compromised by being stepped on; and the skills and confidence to rappel down a two-hundred-foot wall, plus descend a sixty-foot cliff with full rucksack by day or night, whatever the weather. Climbing and descending are both unforgiving activities, and the law of gravity is never suspended just because you're tired or being shot at. You have to do the same thing the same safe way every time. Students also travel to the high peaks of Georgia to practice insertions via helicopter, and make parachute jumps into tiny little drop zones (DZ's) sur-

A Ranger sniper participating in training for jungle warfare. (U.S. Army)

rounded by trees. The lack of sleep and food is continued, and the drop-out rate increases. Injuries are the main reason for dropping out, and in that case the injured can stay around and join the next class unless by then they just want to quit and go home. At every phase the combat patrols grow increasingly complicated, and Opfors (opposing forces) lie in wait to ambush platoons when they least expect it. Then they need to find cover, maintain unit cohesion, and return fire, if not actually attack into the ambushing forces to put them on the defensive. Fast thinking and group dynamics make all the difference.

At a graduation ceremony after his arduous training, a Ranger salutes the drink.
(AP/Racine Journal Times)

The last phase for the survivors is on Day 49, when the now dwindling class goes to Eglin Air Force Base in the Florida panhandle to work on water skills and jungle living. Here they meet the snakes and alligators who live in most jungles, and learn to co-exist with them, eating them when they can. Crossing streams with safety ropes and the use of small rubber boats is also covered here, along with moving through the jungle day after day, either attacking an enemy or else being hunted by the same. Students often begin hallucinating during this phase, either about food or about an enemy who haunts them even as they rest. Only the most determined individuals will make it through to the end, which is a pre-dawn assault by rubber boat on an offshore island.

Only thirty of every one hundred men who start this course will get to the end, but on graduation day, those few can wear their black and gold Ranger tabs proudly, knowing they have the skill and attitude to overcome an unbelievable array of difficulties. More than that, they'll know they can function as the finest light infantry in the world, upholding a tradition that stretches back to the 1600s and is still very much alive today. As true now as it ever was, "Rangers Lead The Way!"

CHAPTER 3

U.S.
Navy
SEALS

When you start to pile on the lengthy list of things that a SEAL has to deal with, you can be forgiven if your head starts to spin and at some point you say: "I don't think I could do all that." The SEALs themselves acknowledge this with a saying popular at their training base in Coronado, California: "The only easy day was yesterday!" But let's not even consider yet their nightmarish schooling. As the U.S. Navy's contribution to Special Operations, SEALs are expected to enter a combat zone in any one of a variety of inconvenient ways, be it parachuting or marching (least preferred) or being dropped off from a rubber raft launched from a submarine. In that case they simply plough their way through waves of large height, then go into the drink and navigate underwater for up to a mile, despite contrary currents and unfriendly sea creatures, and then land on a hostile shore. The thrill of reaching dry land is then mitigated by the need to carry out any of a number of missions, from stealthy reconnaissance to total mayhem, using every high- and low-tech weapon at their disposal. And then somehow they have to extract. Military intelligence isn't any good if you never report back, and you can't go on to retirement if you get zapped somewhere in the bush.

History

Oddly enough, throughout history naval personnel have shown great reluctance to leave their vessels without a darn good reason. After all, that's where the mess hall is, it's your ride home, and it's protected by armor and guns. But there have always been select individuals who thought there was something to be gained by working with the ocean, like the man who built a one-person submarine called *The Turtle* and used it to attach bombs to British vessels in New York harbor during the American Revolution. None of the bombs went off, but he did deploy and carry out a unique mission. During the Civil War,

A member of SEAL Team 2 performs maintenance on a SEAL Delivery Vehicle at the Naval Amphibious Base at Little Creek, Virginia. (DVIC)

Admiral Farragut used (probably unhappy) swimmers to find and neutralize Confederate mines in Mobile Bay. Navy divers were used to try to explain the sinking of the USS *Maine* in Havana Harbor, and again in a number of early submarine mishaps. These divers were of the "hard hat" variety, using long air hoses powered by bellows pumps on their support ships, and were very limited in what they could carry out and how long they could do their work.

But with World War II, that fertile field for special forces, the need for combat swimmers was finally driven home by a series of strategic and tactical considerations. First was the fact that our enemies in both Europe and the Pacific were occupying territory that could best be gotten to through amphibious assaults. Due to the British experience at Gallipoli, this idea was viewed with a great deal of trepidation. In that sorry episode, British, French, and ANZAC troops had failed to get very far off the beaches, and the entire campaign bogged down in a series of fruitless attacks against Turkish defenders. The Allies's first amphibious stab against Nazi Germany—at Dieppe in 1942—was no more encouraging. The Germans destroyed half the landing force and the rest barely got away. As the Allies built up their amphibious capacity it was clear that seaborne landings remained one of the most difficult of all military maneuvers.

It was the disastrous 1943 landing by U.S. Marines at Tarawa in the Pacific that firmly convinced the naval leadership that someone would have to go in ahead of the landing forces to conduct reconnaissance, hydrographic research, clear mines and obstacles, as well as guide in the first waves of assault troops. The landing craft at Tarawa became hung up on uncharted reefs, exposing the Marines to horrific losses from Japanese fire before the beach was anywhere close by. The navy needed small, intrepid units of men who could think on their feet while swimming,

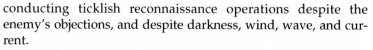

conducting ticklish reconnaissance operations despite the enemy's objections, and despite darkness, wind, wave, and current.

A call went out for volunteers (always a sign that special operations are involved, and a signal to the timid and sensible to steer clear). Originally, men were selected from the dauntless Navy Construction Battalions (Seabees), the Marines, and even (horrors!) the army. These first groups assembled at Fort Pierce, Florida, and began hammering out what would become one of the toughest, and wettest, training regimens of any combat unit. These first groups were called Navy Combat Demolition Units (NCDUs), which morphed into Combat Swimmer Reconnaissance Units and at the end of the war Underwater Demolition Teams (UDTs). The first step was to ensure physical fitness through a series of calisthenics, marches, and runs, and then into the water for all manner of swimming and diving, always with the mission in mind. This meant that prospective NCDU's would have to be adept at propelling themselves through the sea with and without equipment, operating in all sorts of conditions. Diving gear at this time was rudimentary, and it is sad to think that today the average child can walk into K-Mart and buy better masks, snorkels, and flippers than were available to the combat swimmers of 1943. For this reason those early pioneers were known as "Naked Warriors"—not because they didn't desire gear, but because advances in wetsuits, SCUBA, rebreathing, and nitrox were years away from development.

The washout rate was high for these twelve-week training programs, because there just weren't that many people who could handle the grueling instruction coupled with the terrors of working with the ocean in all weather. Invasions were rapidly coming up on the planning tables of the top brass, however, and an experiment was tried with Team 14 in Hawaii. They cut the training time down to six weeks, and though there was still a 40 percent wash-out rate, combat swimmers were available in a much shorter time. Training in Hawaii started each day with a three-and-a-half mile hike to the top of a 9,000-foot mountain, followed by a double-time descent, and then went on to include training with various types of explosives, both the emplacement of and the removal of same. Men were trained to dive to twenty feet and do limited work while holding their breath, as well as how to jump from up to forty-five feet into the ocean. Before being awarded their flippers, candidates were asked to swim a mile in forty-five minutes with no gear. There were also lectures on the various forms of marine life that might be encountered, from the mostly docile manta ray to the deadly sea snakes, and of course the cold-eyed sharks that have ever made men afraid and are attracted especially to the smell of blood.

Local U.S. Marines trained the combat swimmers in judo and hand-to-hand combat, while Seabees shared some of their expertise in creating or destroying all the things to be found on an invasion beach. All manner of explosives were deployed, starting with the satchel charge (simulated by a twenty-pound bag of sand) to the hose charge, which was a long, flexible explosive that could be linked together to clear a path through a minefield. Initially the combat swimmers were trained to jump into the wake of a small landing craft, but this was replaced by a sensible small, rubber boat, which didn't paddle very well and was prone to being knocked about by wind and waves, but was quiet and made a modest target.

The invasion of Saipan was the debut of the combat swimmers, and they conducted a successful reconnaissance in daylight. The Japanese had not caught on to the concept yet. The information brought back by the swimmers concerning the quality of the beach, the obstacles in place, and the nature of the tide were invaluable for the attacking Marines, whose first waves were then led in by selected members of the teams.

At Iwo Jima the Japanese were starting to crack foxy. They employed a series of well-targeted mortars to harass the beach recon teams. Despite the enemy fire, once again the combat swimmers got in and out, and then led the Marines ashore. They also helped clear the beaches after the start of the invasion, a task made more difficult by the fact that Iwo Jima has a steep drop-off just offshore, meaning that damaged craft had a tendency to founder near the beach and block incoming vessels bringing reinforcements and ammunition. But by using pontoon flotation and explosives, the beaches were kept clear despite a hail of shot and shell, and the hard work of clearing the island of enemy troops commenced. The combat swimmers had proven their worth.

NCDUs also participated at D-day in Normandy, losing over 60 percent of their number as casualties on Omaha Beach. Working with army engineers, they frantically tried to destroy hundreds of diabolical German beach obstacles, but due to a slip-up in timing, the first wave of infantry came swarming in before the NCDUs could finish. Infantry instinctively took cover behind the steel obstacles, unaware they had been wired with explosives or were still topped with German mines. Nevertheless, the NCDUs and engineers were able to blast a number of gaps through the obstacles, allowing the invasion to succeed. When the tide went out that afternoon, the remaining obstructions were blown up or bulldozed.

At Okinawa, the teams cleared twelve hundred underwater obstacles in two days under heavy fire without suffering any casualties, which is hard to believe. By the end of the war there were thirty teams consisting of thirty-five hundred men, and the way had been paved for a future of dauntless warriors working offshore, on the beach, and eventually far inland. The U.S. Navy had lit a fire that was to burn brightly to the present day.

In 1947 the various units were consolidated into Underwater Demolition Teams (UDT's), and with the advent of the Korean War (a "police action" that behaved very much like a war), the UDT's were ready once again to participate in their chosen field, as well as branch out a bit. When General Douglas MacArthur pulled off his masterful amphibious invasion of Inchon, UDT's were right there leading the way for the Marines, in a very complicated operation challenged by a monstrous tide and well-defended port emplacements. When U.N. forces were subsequently forced to execute a "retrograde movement" (retreat) by attacking Chinese hordes, UDT's destroyed as much as they could, including an entire port in an orgy of demolition. It was also in Korea that UDT's were tasked with penetrating hostile shores to destroy bridges and tunnels that were close enough to be attacked by a dauntless band from the sea.

After the war, there were always various diving tasks to be done for the navy, including salvage and opening up ports clogged by mines. But as with all Special Operations Forces, peacetime was not good to the UDT's. They had already developed a reputation for working outside channels and coloring outside the lines, and by and large, desk-bound higher officers have never been fond of independent operators.

After President Kennedy announced his strategic vision of a host of small wars in far-off places, the navy decided to form a special unit that could share the enthusiasm that the public was already expressing for the army's Green Berets. In 1962 the first two SEAL teams were created: SEAL Team 1 in the Pacific, and SEAL Team 2 in the Atlantic. SEAL stands for Sea-Air-Land, and is meant to convey not only the aquatic portion of their mission, but also the fact that they were being developed into a "do anything, go anywhere" unit for a new type of warfare. Their first assignments came when NASA had to deal with returning space capsules, which landed with fair precision in the Pacific and then had to be stabilized by flotation collars so that the returning astronauts wouldn't sink to the bottom. The men doing the attaching of the collars were Navy SEALs.

But it was during the Vietnam War that the SEALs really took off. Though they maintained a low profile at the time, enough has come out since to inspire awe in their achievements. While the army, Marines, and air force—whether on the conventional or special operations side—emerged from the war the worse for wear, it was the Navy SEALs who most seemed to understand their theater of operations and to make it their own in a way that still resonates. They began by putting in a few men in 1962, and then a few teams by 1965.

In Vietnam the SEALs, though a specialized elite, were never the object of enmity or envy from fellow soldiers. That's because no one else wanted to do what they were doing. Their main stomping ground was the Mekong Delta south of Saigon, an unholy tangle of streams, canals, islands, jungles, and swamps, with no end of snakes (including cobras up to eighteen feet long), insects, leeches, crocodiles, and the occasional tiger thrown in for good measure. There was a hot season that sweltered, and a rainy season that made everything turn into mud. Plus there was the Viet Cong.

The SEAL teams were given great autonomy by their commanders, and they used it for all it was worth, running their own intelligence and planning many of their own missions. They had the "brown water navy" consisting of PBR's and Swift boats for transportation and firepower, and they could call in air force jets and their own "Sea Wolf" helicopters if they had to get away in a hurry or have somebody lay down some withering cover fire. A

In South Vietnam in January 1969, SEALs observe the effect of a satchel charge they have just planted to blow up a Viet Cong bunker. (AP)

SEAL team could consist of up to fourteen men, but seven or eight was the norm, and those seven or eight carried enough firepower to impose their will on vastly superior numbers of Viet Cong (VC). Tactically, the indigenous VC quickly lost any edge they might have possessed. The SEALs became experts at night ops, ambushes, combat recon, prisoner snatches, and raids. Typically they would decide on a target, usually a place where the VC were passing through, and then would start out just after dark, deploy stealthily before midnight, hit the enemy as hard as they could, and be home for debriefing by dawn.

In places like the Rung-Sat Special Zone, the "devils with green faces" (as the VC called them for their face paint) pulled off a lengthy list of hair-raising adventures that still give one the chills. By using speed, surprise, stealth, fire discipline, and an irrepressible spirit of "Can do!" the SEALs were able to take the war to the enemy in a way that seemed to belie the sputtering results of the broader war. The SEALs also learned a few new tricks, such as safe cracking to steal enemy documents, the use of silenced pistols for guard dogs (called "hush puppies"), and they experimented with weapons like the Stoner system and flechettes. The Stoner was a brilliantly designed rifle that could be made into various configurations, including a short machine gun—but it was temperamental, an undesirable quality in combat. Flechettes are ammunition in the form of tiny darts, useful for ricochet through heavy ground cover. Most of the SEALs' firepower, however, consisted of standard M-16's, M-60 machine guns with a short barrel, the standard grenade launchers, and old-fashioned but always relevant shotguns.

On a mission, the drill was to travel about twenty miles by boat, as fast as possible, and then to slow down and begin a slower cruise near where the team wanted to be. Then, instead of firing off flares and putting up a sign, the team would slip over the

A Navy SEAL practicing a ship takedown at sea. He is using an MP-5 submachine gun.

side and crawl up on the bank. Waiting to make sure the PBR was clear while listening for unfriendly noises, the team would then quietly make their way to their destination, with each man watching an assigned quadrant, and the point man in the lead forging ahead. If they were ambushed, they were trained to attack into the ambush, surely a counterintuitive tactic, but an effective one, going back to Roger's Rangers. When the first enemy gun fired, the men of the trident would unleash a devastating response, using every weapon at their disposal. When traveling, the last man in line would sweep the trail to prevent their being followed, and also listen for any pursuing enemy.

They would also often leave a booby trap behind for anybody with too much interest in who they were and where they were going.

It was in Vietnam that the SEALs forged a strong bond with their boat crews, known as SBS (Special Boat Squadrons), who had the unenviable task of navigating the SEALs to their chosen area and then picking them up at the end of the evening's festivities, often under withering fire. The boats were noisy and prime candidates for ambush, but many of their captains were among the finest boat-handlers in the navy. And with their .50-caliber twins up front, and a grenade launcher and M-60 on the stern, a PBR could hold its own in firefights..

At the end of the Vietnam War, the SEALs made sure to keep in mind all the things they had learned at such high cost. They had made the hellhole swamps and rivers their own, beating the enemy at their own game, and had forged the template for the modern teams. They also broadened out to include intelligence gathering, counterterrorism operations, strategic raids, and working with the locals.

By the time the invasion of Grenada, Operation Urgent Fury, took place in 1983, a new generation of SEALs was highly trained but yet untested in combat conditions. They were to do a recon of two places: Point Salines at the southwest corner of the island, and an airfield farther north. The Point Salines operation went tragically wrong for a number of the units involved, but it was especially harsh for four SEALs who were drowned offshore in an overly complicated nighttime drop of men and militarized Boston Whalers. Farther north, the SEALs were able to report that the beaches were unsuitable for the planned Marine invasion, saving many lives when helicopters were used instead. But then, there were radio mix-ups, equipment failures, more resistance from the defenders than expected, and other signs that the

SEALs were rusty, and that their commanders needed to think through their missions more carefully.

But there were enough mishaps in Grenada to spread around the entire special operations community, and the positive result was SOCOM, Special Operations Command, which was activated in 1987. When the crisis in Panama occurred two years later, America's elite forces were better prepared.

During Operation Just Cause, the invasion of Panama, SEALs were given the priority tasks of destroying General Manuel Noriega's private ship (a converted patrol boat) and his jet aircraft. The ship was blown up by two two-man teams of swimmers in a harrowing operation. While the SEALs planted demolitions on the craft beneath the surface, Panamanian soldiers on the piers above—suspecting something was up—tossed grenades in the water. The swimmers extricated safely, having to dive fifty feet beneath a passing cargo ship to join their waiting teammates.

At the airport that housed Noriega's private jet, things did not go so smoothly. SEAL officers had suggested that the plane be disabled by a small infiltration team, or even by a sniper team placed in a building overlooking the hangar. Instead a three-platoon raid was launched. The SEALs reached the coastal airfield undetected in fifteen rubber boats, only to face a 1,500-yard approach to the hangar across a flat, illuminated runway overlooked by buildings on all sides. Worse, firing had already broken out in the city and Panamanian troops at the airfield were now alert and waiting.

It being difficult for SEALs to camouflage themselves on a concrete runway, they were met by a torrent of fire from three directions as they reached the hangar. A dozen Americans went down, four dead and eight wounded. But in this OK Corral style of battle, SEAL courage and firepower soon got the upper hand.

 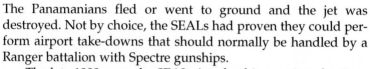

The Panamanians fled or went to ground and the jet was destroyed. Not by choice, the SEALs had proven they could perform airport take-downs that should normally be handled by a Ranger battalion with Spectre gunships.

The late 1980s saw the SEALs involved in a series of actions in the Persian Gulf, involving all manner of operations against Iranians who were bent on disrupting the flow of oil to the West. They used two huge oil-tender barges as floating bases within which were concealed SEAL small boats and helicopters. The SEALs played cat and mouse with Iranian craft that sallied out at night to lay mines or attack tankers, boarding or sinking Iranian craft when necessary. These operations concluded with the end of the Iran-Iraq War.

A member of SEAL Team 8 manning an M-60 machine gun on a firing range in Kuwait. (DVIC)

In 1991 during Desert Storm, the SEALs were able to carry out a grand deception on the beaches of Iraq. It convinced Saddam Hussein that there was to be a full amphibious operation coming ashore in the near future—while the army made its famous left hook through the desert and crushed the Iraqi forces. By their dangerous hydrographic missions in chilly fifty-degree water, the SEALs made an impact out of all proportion to their numbers.

In 2001 in Afghanistan, U.S. Navy SEALs were part of the unprecedented triumph of Special Operations Forces in destroying Taliban and Al Qaeda forces in Afghanistan. Working as part of a well-unified team, their still-classified actions have only come out in dribs and drabs, but have involved targeting ground positions for bombardment from the air, and patrolling the rugged terrain in search of a wily enemy. One SEAL died fighting Al Qaeda at Shah-i-Kot. What were SEALs doing waging combat in the eastern mountains of a landlocked country, hundreds of miles from the sea, you might ask? A bigger question would have been how to have kept them out of that war.

Training

Becoming a Navy SEAL has the reputation of being one of the worst processes for which any soldier can volunteer. The training is uncompromisingly tough, and the washout rate is high. Instead of the six weeks that the UDT's in Hawaii endured in World War II, SEAL training has now expanded to twenty-six weeks at Coronado, California, where the cold Pacific rolls in powerful breakers, and the sugary sand and pounding sun are the only relief from the instructor's voice.

To start with, recruits have to be in the U.S. Navy, not more than twenty-eight-years-old, have a good record, and their eyesight has to be at least 20/40 in one eye and no worse than 20/70 in the other, correctable with lenses. Then they have to do an ungodly amount of paperwork to make sure they are healthy and can withstand a few dives, and some running, and some swimming. The minimum physical requirements are that they be able to swim five hundred yards sidestroke in twelve and a half minutes, run one and a half miles in boots and pants in eleven and a half minutes, and do forty-two push-ups in two minutes, fifty sit-ups in two minutes, and six pull-ups. Go out and try that some afternoon if you want to look at the SEAL trident insignia in a whole new light. And those are just the requirements to get into BUD/S, the Basic Underwater Demolition/Swimmer portion of SEAL training, which is just the first five weeks.

During those first weeks, the time is spent doing calisthenics, negotiating the obstacle course, swimming in the ocean, and learning to work with a team. But rather than spend a lot of time and money on those without the intestinal fortitude to see the whole thing through, the third week is "Hell Week." During this time the recruits operate in the surf and onshore twenty-four hours a day, with no more than four hours sleep for the whole week. Here's where the whole "cold/wet/tired" matrix of spoilers comes through loud and clear. They can quit at any time by ringing a little bell mounted on a post, or just by throwing their helmet to the ground as hard as they can. But those who have what it takes will somehow persist, and get to the end of this period knowing they are already a long ways removed from the average Joe on the street. For the survivors of Hell Week, there is much to be learned about hydrographic surveying techniques (just as the UDTs before them) and basic seamanship. The 400-pound rubber rafts are carried everywhere, as instructors hate to waste any teachable moments. And much time is spent in the surf, getting colder and colder.

The second phase of BUD/S consists of diving training; both

open circuit (using compressed air as civilian divers do) and closed circuit (using recycled oxygen that doesn't leave any tell-tale bubbles). The times required in the four-mile run and two mile swim are lowered, but in their place come academic tasks on which they must score well (80 percent and higher for officers; 70 percent and higher for enlisted men) or go home. Diving is an inherently unsafe activity, as risky as parachuting or climbing, and a moment's inattention can have grave consequences. It's a finicky and precise sport, and when you take it into a combat environment you need to be as heads-up as possible. Underwater navigation and beach reconnaissance are part of this phase as well.

Phase three is land warfare, because where they are going there will be hostile locals ashore who mean them harm. Here the navy improves on the traditional landing party that naval ships have put ashore throughout history, in that SEALs need to be experts at land navigation, small-unit tactics, rappelling, and explosives, both on land and at sea. And to hone their skills further, four weeks are spent on San Clemente Island in practical exercises designed to help these frogmen transition to the shore in the most deadly fashion possible. And then they've graduated from BUD/S.

But they are not SEALs yet. There's a six-month probationary period, and then they are cleared to go on to graduate schools and be assigned to a SEAL team. Then they can wear the famous insignia of an eagle holding a trident and a pistol, the well-known mark of the U.S. Navy SEAL. Graduate schools include a dizzying array of options, such as Airborne training with the army at Fort Benning, SEAL Delivery Vehicle (SDV) school (three months), as well as learning how to work with their new team and gain proficiency at the wide array of skills needed to be one of the elite.

Navy SEALs practice assaulting a ground hole, such as were prevalent in Vietnam and also in Afghanistan. (DVIC)

They begin their weapons training early and continue as long as they are SEALs, because shooting skills degrade rapidly. The main tools are the Beretta 9mm semi-automatic pistol, the M-16A2 rifle, the Squad Automatic Weapon (SAW), the M-60 machine gun, and the M-79 grenade launcher, a handy breech-loaded single shot that allows them to express 40mm grenade feelings out to 380 yards—artillery for the individual. Fancy knives for diving and fighting may be issued, but most soldiers use them for cooking. More upscale weaponry is introduced, such as the Heckler & Koch P95 pistol and the H&K MP-5 submachine gun, beautifully made and accurate guns. SEALs also use the Colt 727, called the "CAR 15" 5.56mm rifle, which is a shortened version of the M16, with the M203 44mm grenade launcher tucked underneath the barrel. If there's a more versatile combination of firepower out there than the above, I'm sure the SEALs will find it. SEAL teams may also avail themselves of the Sig Sauer P226 9mm pistol, the old Colt .45, or even .357 Magnum revolvers, because they have the discretion and the armory to use whatever will get the job done. And that includes the Mossberg shotguns and the Winchester 700 bolt-action rifle for sniping.

In an exercise near Hawaii, a SEAL fast-ropes from a Seahawk helicopter to rendezvous with a nuclear sub, which has just surfaced to the right. (DVIC)

All manner of things that blow up are second nature to a SEAL, from satchel charges to the innocent looking block of C-4, which can be molded around metal parts, to the Claymore mine, which can be rigged as perimeter defense or used as a booby-trap on the back-trail. The array of grenades covers the waterfront from fragmentation to smoke to white phosphorous (WP), which burns at two thousand degrees anywhere it ignites, including underwater.

Basic navigation is done with topographical maps, nautical charts, aviation charts, aerial photographs, and any other piece of paper, including foreign maps. The basic Silva compass, beloved of civilian orienteers, is used for its bombproof construction. And any time they think their compass is in error, it's generally time to rethink their navigation. Hand-held GPS units are used as a back-up, but batteries can go dead—it is better to be able to track themselves with the old map and compass. And don't forget the radios, the PRC-117 for talking to their commanders, and the MX-300 UHF for talking to the rest of their team.

SEALs also have the hands-down best ways of moving around the landscape (and seascape), whether by locking out of a submarine with SCUBA gear, or driving the Desert Patrol Vehicle (DPV) which comes with a .50-caliber machine gun, small rockets, and a 20mm Gatling gun. On the ocean, the teams and their drivers use everything from small rubber rafts to hopped-up Zodiacs, including the new SEAL Delivery Vehicle Mark V, which is a 50-knot, 80-foot, low-to-the-water bruiser that can carry an entire SEAL team and all its gear, as well as shoot the crap out of anything it runs into.

In peacetime, SEAL Team 1 is responsible for southern Asia outside of China and Korea. SEAL Teams 2 and 5 are trained for arctic warfare. SEAL Team 4 is the woodland/jungle team. The various deserts are the AO (area of operations) for SEAL Teams 3

Secretary of Defense Donald Rumsfeld receives a briefing on the latest SEAL equipment in November 2001, during a visit to Pope Air Force Base, North Carolina. (Dept. of Defense)

and 8. Antiterrorist and hostage rescue is done by SEAL Team 6, which also annoyingly penetrates U.S. military bases world-wide on a real-time basis with no warning. These exercises result in quite a few red faces.

But in wartime, the SEALs will do what they have always done: show up where they're least expected, and perform missions in a way that will astound and absolutely slay their opponents. Unless they're asked to do a "sneak and peek;" in which case you won't even know they were there.

CHAPTER 4

U.S.
Air Force
Special
Operations

Some people are nervous to fly. Believe it or not, even more are wary of flying "nape of the earth"—fifty feet off the ground to avoid enemy radar—dodging power lines, trees or minarets, susceptible at any moment to antiaircraft fire or missiles. And a tremendous amount of people are hesitant to dive out of an aircraft into enemy territory, using their combat, communications and rescue skills to coordinate the world's most hi-tech hardware with the sweat and guts of operators on the ground. The tension alone, of knowing that the mission and the lives of other American soldiers will depend on the perfection of your performance, would not be welcome to many citizens.

But fortunately we have U.S. Air Force Special Operations. Tactically, this unique breed of warriors provides our operatives behind-the-lines logistics and striking power; strategically they guarantee our capacity to project force into any nook or cranny of the globe, in any light or weather. If the "sun never set" on the maritime British Empire, neither the sun, moon, nor stars inhibit the global reach of USAF SpecOps. If Britannia ruled the waves,

America owns the sky. With a heritage that goes back to World War II but having a dedicated role only since the early 1960s, the "Air Commandos" have been able to build a capability of staggering dimensions with very little notice from the public or press. But they are the reason why other Special Operations Forces can have impact around the world, anywhere, at any time.

The air force version of Special Operations is composed of talented and dedicated soldiers with an astonishing variety and depth of training; men who can deal with the nuts and bolts of being isolated in heavy combat on the ground while also being able to master the entire range of modern technology, from transport to fire support to weather to navigation to intelligence gathering and target designation. They are also masters of Search & Rescue (SAR), and its lively Combat cousin (CSAR), and routinely deploy that curious hybrid the Pararescue Jumper (PJ), who cannot only shoot you to pieces, but also patch you up and extract you in jig time.

AFSOC has become a vital link between the commandos on the ground and the resources of the most powerful air force in history. This means they cannot only find you a place to land heavy cargo planes, but they can also rain hell from above with gunships and laser-designated bombs and missiles. They not only deliver operators into strategically vital danger zones, but deposit their own men to direct a fearless stream of back-up. The combination of technological and combat skills, not to mention raw courage, required of Air Commandos makes them among the most complex and well-trained of all Special Operations Forces.

History

After World War I there was a brief period when military theorists predicted the supremacy of air power, opining that future wars would be decided by long-range, high-level aircraft alone.

A member of the Air Force SpecOps Special Tactics Group in training at Pope Air Force Base, Louisiana. (U.S. Air Force)

World War II put paid to this concept as fighters and flak decimated bomber streams, while newly mobile armor, infantry, and artillery achieved the only true results on the ground. Nevertheless, air mobility added a new dimension to the conflict—not only spreading its scale but allowing a surprise behind-the-lines capability.

In the sweltering jungles of the Pacific Theater in 1943, one of the great screwballs of military history decided he needed a new kind of air support for his new kind of fighting force. That man was Orde Wingate, the legendary bible-toting commando leader who formed the "Chindits" for the British to harass and bedevil the Japanese in Burma. The Chindits's specialty was to insert by parachute or Waco glider behind Japanese lines and then fight their way back to safety. They were followed by Merrill's Marauders, American raiders who marched into enemy territory

The founders of the U.S. Air Commandos in World War II, Colonels John Allison and Phil Cochran, flank the eccentric British General Orde Wingate. The Air Commandos were first formed to support the operations of Wingate's Chindit raiders in Burma.

to create as much havoc as they could. These operations strongly resembled those of Confederate raiders in the Civil War west; except in World War II, as Wingate recommended, the raids could now be supported by additional raiders from the air.

In August 1943, U.S. Army Air Corps General Henry "Hap" Arnold, after a meeting with Lord Louis Mountbatten (former head of British commandos and by then commander in chief of the Burma theater) ordered the creation of Project 9, an air support group for the Allied raiders. This outfit, renamed the 1st Air Commando Group the following year, was formed by Colonels John Allison and Phil Cochran. Arnold stressed that he did not want to hear about paperwork but only missions and results, with the two colonels able to draw upon any equipment or crews they wished. From the beginning they ran an innovative outfit, partly by choice and partly by circumstance. They not only operated in an area with terrible weather and poor maps (later to become the province of the CIA's Air America), but they also used some of the first operational helicopters for both CSAR and aerial assault. After a crash during a training mission, the British officer in command reassured the Americans that his men would still fly with them "any place, any time, anywhere," providing the Air Commandos a motto that remains to this day. In Burma, the Air Commandos got as down and dirty as the raiders, flying at low-level through Japanese air space, backing up the troops with firepower or supplies, extracting wounded from carved-out airfields while delivering reinforcements or food. These hazardous missions inside the tiger's mouth achieved far more than any high-level carpet bombing of the jungle.

At the same time in Europe, the "Carpetbaggers" of the 801st Bombardment Group were performing dangerous low-level missions over Nazi-held territory. These involved dropping OSS commandos and providing further support in nocturnal deliveries. To provide a perspective on these missions, the gospel of regular Air Corps crews was to depend on formation flying, for the ability to aim 540 machine guns within a tight group of thirty-nine planes against German interceptors. If a plane broke off from the formation it was considered to be at high risk, if not done for. The SpecOps guys purposely invaded the continent solo, flying beneath the enemy radar screen—though vulnerable to the enemy's ground-spotter network—in the teeth of the Germans's highly developed nightfighter arm. These daring aviators supported partisan units from France and Norway to Yugoslavia. They used modified, black-painted B-24 Liberators for personnel drops, as well as the hardy C-47 Dakota for drops and supply.

The Air Commandos were disbanded after World War II but the concept was soon resurrected. During the Korean War, the newly separate Air Force (formed in 1947) used covert planes to both drop agents behind the lines and directly attack enemy fuel depots with homemade bomb racks and napalm. But it was in Vietnam that air force Special Operations began to take on their modern appearance. Starting in 1961, the USAF began fighting in a new way, one that included not only CSAR and transport, but also aggressive new platforms such as "Puff the Magic Dragon"—a C-47 made into a flying gun platform, the AC-47. This carried a 3-gun battery of the amazing General Electric minigun (built on the Gatling principle of revolving barrels not seen since the turn of the century, but now powered instead of hand-cranked) which could send ammo downrange at an astonishing six thousand rounds per minute.

Not surprisingly, the disposal of empty shell casings was a problem, but airborne housekeeping issues were nothing compared to the world of hurt visited upon their targets. Clever pilots figured out a way to "orbit" a target so that the miniguns (which pointed out of one side of the plane) would always be trained upon a plot of land on the ground. This would quickly be filled with holes, as would whatever enemy forces who tried to hide there. Also known as "Spooky" (for obvious reasons), these visionary new air support squadrons saved many a ground unit out of range of their own artillery and knee-deep in human waves of Viet Cong. Isolated Green Beret A-teams on hilltops and Marine companies on patrol all benefited from "Spooky." Soon the C-130 Hercules, that venerable four-engine transport, was being pressed into service and the miniguns were joined by larger guns up to and including a 105mm howitzer, which normal

The famous "Puff the Magic Dragon," an AC-47 flown by Air Commandos during the Vietnam War. The father of today's AC-130 Spectre gunships, its port side bristled with weapons which could remain concentrated on the target as the pilot circled above.

people would hesitate to mount on an aircraft. The modern AC-130 Spectre is still considered the best friend of any Special Operations unit, because it can fire "danger close" to friendly troops while dropping an absolute curtain of steel and explosive shells directly where it's needed the most: right in the enemy's wheelhouse.

Also making their debut in Vietnam were such workhorses as the Chinook, the Huey, and the Jolly Green Giant—all helicopters that went on to have storied careers as combat aircraft capable of fairly high speeds as well as the ability to hover and touch down anywhere the pilot thought it was a good idea. The Chinook is a twin-rotor transport helicopter that can carry over forty men and their gear; the Huey is a single rotor unit that came to symbolize the entire war and was used for "dust-offs" as well as transport (the transport versions were called "slicks" to differentiate them from the gunship type); and the Jolly Green Giant is the massive HH-3 (later updated to the HH-53) that was used to drop troops off and perform CSAR. The HH-53 carried two miniguns and a hoist with 250 feet of steel cable that could be let down through the jungle canopy and used to extract a downed pilot by seating him on the "jungle penetrator" before winching him to safety.

The men who often went down these cables to the downed pilots were the Pararescue Jumpers (PJs), highly-trained combat medics who are also heavily armed. It was in Vietnam that the air rescue service really came into its own, running hundreds of missions of mercy, as well as being able to penetrate forbidden air space such as over Laos, Cambodia, and North Vietnam. If a pilot or an SOG team was in trouble on the ground, the Jolly Green Giant and its dauntless crew were their best chance to sleep in a bunk that night. But for all the effort, innovation, and experience the new Air Commandos gained in Vietnam, not to mention the

Air Force Pararescue Jumpers fast-rope from an HH-53 Jolly Green Giant. The HH-53, first used during Vietnam, has since been upgraded with navigation, sensor and weapons technology. (U.S. Air Force)

blood and courage they freely revealed, the entire effort, strategically, came to naught.

After Vietnam, the Air Force joined the rest of the U.S. military in the great funk, with cutbacks, drastic drops in force levels, and low morale. But they were rudely shaken out of it in 1980 with the Desert One disaster in Iran. That gallant attempt to rescue American hostages was embarrassingly betrayed by its aviation elements. First, the navy pilots of eight Sea Stallion helicopters hadn't been trained for overland operations so they were replaced by Marine pilots. But the Marines hadn't been trained in nocturnal, low-level desert flying either. Second, two copters malfunctioned and turned back; two more sat out a sandstorm on the ground while the disoriented remainder flew through the storm. Upon arriving at the secret airfield over an hour late, another Sea Stallion indicated a cracked rotor blade. Now down to five helicopters, the mission had to be aborted. Finally, disappointment turned to catastrophe when a helicopter accidentally collided with a C-130 cargo aircraft and both exploded, killing eight Americans. The site was abandoned, leaving bodies, wreckage, and intact helicopters (with secret papers and equipment) for the Iranians to find in the morning.

Tragic as it was, Desert One can be considered the birthplace of the new U.S. focus on Special Operations Forces, exceeding that which occurred during Kennedy's presidency in the early 1960s. If the United States was going to stop staring at its navel and resume its role as a superpower, the first priority was reestablishing a global tactical capacity through aviation.

But the real heavy lifting for the United States to firm up its global reach had to come from the USAF. In March 1983, all Air Force Special Operations were transferred from the 23rd Air Force in Illinois and based at Hurlburt Field, Florida, as the 1st Special Operations Wing. The 1st SOW was equipped with the "130"

Night Stalkers

The army's reaction to the tragedy of Desert One was to create a new specialized unit using crack helicopter pilots from its 101st Airborne Division. Designated the 160th Special Operations Aviation Regiment (SOAR), it was equipped with long-range, twin-rotored Chinooks, refuelable Black Hawks and Pave Hawks and, most recently, highly versatile Little Birds. In the past two decades U.S. electronics have made quantum leaps beyond what was available in 1980 and today Special Operations aircraft are equipped with forward-looking infrared scanners, terrain-following radar, advanced navigation, evasion, countermeasure, and communications systems. And they also pack a lot of firepower. SOAR can be seen as the integral aviation arm of the Army Rangers, Special Forces, and Delta. Most of its helicopters are painted black, providing a clue as to why they make U.S. opponents uneasy. They operate after dark as easily as other craft do during the day. Thus the men of the 160th are commonly known as the "Night Stalkers."

An MH-53J Pave Low helicopter of the 58th Special Operations Wing. The Pave Low, packed with the latest in weapons and electronic gadgetry, would have made a huge difference had it been available at Desert One in Iran. (U.S. Air Force)

series of aircraft, including Spectre gunships, Combat Talons, refueling and AWACs planes. Its rotary line-up featured the "53" series of Pave Low and Jolly Green Giant helicopters, capable of long-range transport, CSAR, or serving as gunships. For long-range missions or any other tasks that the high command desired, USAF SpecOps would provide the means. American air power might still appear in the public's mind as "top gun" fighter pilots or bomber crews in increasingly exotic aircraft. But now the Air Commandos were back: men and their craft ready to mix it up at low-level in enemy territory, supporting our most daring operatives.

Air Force Special Operations has two aspects: the Special Tactics Group, consisting of commandos who need to accompany and hold their own with Special Forces, SEALs, or anyone else in ground, airborne, or water operations, plus be geniuses of technical knowledge, judgment and clarity in order to liaison with the craft aloft; and the pilots and crewmen of the aircraft. As Air Force Special Operations got going in the 1980s there was not at first a strong identification among the fliers as Special Operations troops. It was more a matter of "If you crew a Spectre, you're SpecOps; if you crew a B-52, you're not." But this began to change as operational tempo increased and crews grew accustomed to flying special missions in tandem with other operators.

The invasion of Grenada in October 1983 indicated room for improvement across the entire SOF spectrum. But the problems only created more impetus for change. Special Operations Command came into being in 1987, tying together air force, army, and navy Special Operations resources under a unified command. By the time the invasion of Panama took place in 1989, the air force was into the Special Operations world with a vengeance. In the air, it delivered troops wherever they wanted to go while laying down devastating, accurate fire when requested. On the ground, Combat Control Teams accompanied the operators, providing liaison with the birds up top for fire support, reconnaissance, resupply, or extractions. PJs became a routine part of any combat operation, CSAR was a carefully planned and complex mission, and AC-130s were expected to be orbiting in the skies overhead.

In May 1990, Air Force Special Operations Command was activated at Hurlburt Field with three SpecOps Wings (one based in the UK and one in Japan) and one Special Tactics Group, over twelve thousand men in all. The following year, Air Force SpecOps craft kicked off Desert Storm, the allied counteroffensive against Saddam Hussein. In the dead of night on January 17,

During the war in Afghanistan, an Air Force SpecOps Combat Controller patrols the vicinity of his helicopter, which has landed in Northern Alliance territory. (AP)

1991, flights of Pave Low helicopters led Army Apaches into Iraq. Flying "nape of the earth," the Pave Lows guided the attackers to two Iraqi radar stations, which were then obliterated by Hellfire missiles. This broke open an air corridor into Iraq through which over 850 U.S. and coalition aircraft attacked that day.

During the rest of Desert Storm, Air Force Special Operations craft performed a variety of missions. Combat Talons neutralized Iraqi minefields with 15,000-pound bombs while Spectres neutralized Iraqi troops with their mini-guns and howitzers. On the ground, Air Force operators accompanied A-teams (and sometimes SAS) into the countryside or performed Direct Action and reconnaissance missions of their own. On January 31, AF SpecOps suffered the coalition's worst air loss when a Spectre gunship went down with all fourteen crewmen. The AC-130 had just destroyed an Iraqi battery in support of the Marines's battle at Khafji when it was hit by a surface-to-air missile and crashed in the Persian Gulf.

In 2001 and 2002 in Afghanistan, air force operators were once more in the vanguard, covertly inserted into the country to direct the U.S. airstrikes that brought the Taliban to its knees. The Special Operations crews above meanwhile performed such missions as delivering huge "daisy cutter" bombs to destroy the cave complexes on which Osama bin Laden and his minions had counted for refuge. While air force and navy fighters crisscrossed the skies and majestic bombers crossed half the world to deliver their payloads, USAF Special Operations Forces filled in the gaps around the Hindu Kush, connecting U.S. air power to the war on the ground.

Training

The pilots and crews of AF Special Operations are among the most daring and skilled in the Air Force. Further, they possess that intangible willingness, common to all SpecOps forces, to introduce themselves to risk rather than wait for its acquaintance. Air Commandos see less of the "wild blue yonder" than they see of the jungles, deserts, woods, or mountains, where operators need insertion, extraction, logistics, firepower, or aid, under the very noses of the enemy. But while the SpecOps flyboys are a breed apart, the Combat Controllers and Pararescue Jumpers they drop from their aircraft add a whole new dimension to the word "capable." These guys not only need to possess the skills of any other SpecOps soldier but then some.

As with the rest of the Special Operations Forces, recruits for the Air Force Special Tactics Group—the ground operators— have to really, really want the job. And they need to demonstrate

AF Special Operations troops participate in the combat weapons portion of a competition called the Defender Challenge near San Antonio in 1999. The week-long contest between SOF troops results in an award called the Sadler Cup. (AP)

it by going through a training regimen that beggars belief. It all starts at the notoriously sultry Lackland Air Force Base in Texas, where they fly a black warning flag on the few days deemed to be too hot to conduct physical exercise. It is here that the PAST (Physical Abilities and Stamina Test) are conducted. First is a twenty-five-meter underwater swim, during which you fail if you surface. Then the one-thousand-meter surface swim, where you fail if you pause. Then the mile-and-a-half run, which must be done in under ten and a half minutes, and a series of chin-ups, sit-ups, pull-ups, and flutter kicks. Any male officer or enlisted man in the Air Force can take this test, but few can make it all the way through. You also need three letters of recommendation from superior officers, and have to write an essay on why, for you, this all seems like a good idea. Twelve weeks of hell at the Indoctrination Course await the lucky winners, usually about 25 percent of those who apply.

The Special Tactics Squadrons would like to have just a little over a year to turn out exceptional commandos who can do everything under the sun, as well as at night, underwater, and in combat. For this reason the training is sometimes called "Superman University." But as with so many other modern

SpecOps Forces, sheer muscle and guts alone are not enough to ensure passing through this grueling period and emerging to wear the maroon beret of USAF Special Operations. They are looking for men who cannot only outlast, outfight, and out-shoot the enemy, but also men who can outmaneuver and out-think a foe. Football linemen and bruising boneheads are not what they're after. Better throw a good brain in your rucksack before you get to Lackland, one that is flexible and creative, and combine that with an iron will and sharp wits.

The first two weeks are reputedly all physical training as recruits are brought up to the standards expected of modern warriors. Endless running and push-ups form the basic routine, and they are also watched and evaluated at every step of the way by instructors who by no means wish to pass everyone. Recruits can always be thrown out at any step along the way. The third week is "motivational week," which the instructors interpret as less food, less sleep, less rest, and more stress. In this way it's not too different from "Hell Week" during BUD/S training for Navy SEALs. Up to nine out of ten drop out during this stage. The survivors receive training in shooting, land navigation, and all of the skills that one would expect of prospective combatants. Complicated tasks are required in a variety of inconvenient settings, and no excuses are tolerated. From there it's on to the U.S. Army's Combat Divers School in Key West where candidates are trained in all of the modern SCUBA techniques, including the Draeger rebreather which allows one to swim around without trailing a stream of bubbles.

Then comes a series of classes from the U.S. Navy on how to exit aircraft which have crashed in the water, and if you haven't been shaken yet this ought to do the trick. Men are blindfolded and strapped into a mock helicopter that plunges into a tank of water and rolls upside down, at which point they are free to see if they can get unstrapped and find the surface, where the air is kept. (If they find the air they pass.) This is followed by three weeks of parachute training at Fort Benning to earn their jump wings, which both the SEALs and the AFSOC guys seem to find relaxing for some reason, and then the thrilling U.S. Army Military Freefall Parachutist School at Fort Bragg, North Carolina. In a freefall you get to exit the plane (often at high altitude) and fall like a stone at 180 feet per second and fly your way into a drop zone, pausing only to pull the ripcord when you've reached a height that seems low to observers. By this method men can be infiltrated almost invisibly into almost any place on earth, because the plane dropping them off can fly so high as to

Master Sergeant Kenneth Taylor from the Special Operations Squadron "flies" the Visual Threat Recognition and Avoidance Trainer (VTRAT) that he designed. This device allows pilots and crewmen continuing practice in how to identify and avoid different types of ground fire in a combat zone. (U.S. Air Force)

be inaudible on the ground, and men falling don't make good visual or radar targets. All it takes is steely nerves.

Yuma, Arizona, is where prospects hone their freefall skills, and then the trackless wilderness of Washington State is next for an immersion in the sort of northern forest that covers much of the world. Here men learn to make fire and shelter, as well as how to ascend tall mountains in all weather and descend cliffs by means of rappelling. You can see the theme here: recruits must be able to operate in the air, on the ground, underwater, in jungles, on mountains, in deserts, and anywhere else there is likely to be combat; and in today's world that means anywhere on earth, from downtown New York to the Hindu Kush.

For those wishing to be PJs, the beginning is the standard Special Operations Combat Medic Course at Fort Bragg. This means twenty-four weeks of dealing with all manner of trauma in the field, from hangnails to head wounds. Candidates learn every facet of emergency medicine from the standard SOAP note and ABC (airway, breathing, circulation) to more advanced techniques such as intubation and the proper use of medications in the field. They may do a month-long rotation in a crime-ridden city, exposing them to a nightmare of injuries and an endless stream of victims. Then they get a three-phase turn at the Pararescue Recovery Specialist course, which first focuses on field work and all the advanced ways to move around the landscape in a hostile environment, and then goes to the medical phase where they learn about every bit of rescue gear a man can carry. And then there is the phase where they become familiar with all the aircraft they may encounter in their careers, as well as how to use them, leave them, rejoin them, and saw them apart to rescue others after they've crashed. They will also do SCUBA jumps into water, and tree jumps into, well, trees. This is always deemed unwise by parachutists, but PJs may have to do it so they are given a special protective suit (padded in the groin and armpits and with a special helmet) that also includes enough rope to be able to climb down from a tree 150-feet high (as tall as a fifteen-story building).

All PJs carry the same medical kit packed just the same way, so they can use another man's kit quickly if they have to, or use it at night by feel. The PJs are among the most highly-trained and motivated individuals you could ever hope to meet, and their ability to kill and heal is a curious amalgamation of skills that is thoroughly modern, and put together, as their motto puts it, "That Others May Live." One crucial distinction between PJs and the standard "street" EMT is that the latter is taught to protect himself first and to survey the scene carefully before just wading in and becoming another victim, such as in the case of a person who has been electrocuted. With PJs, they are well aware of danger and survey the scene with the best of them, but then they rush in anyway, turn off the power, help the victim, and are prepared to shoot the repair guy when he shows up to fix the line. They will be asked to go into combat zones and not behave as feckless nurses, but rather as vital combatants themselves who can also stabilize and transport the wounded and do it while emptying as many clips as it takes to provide a therapeutic recovery area for their patients.

The men who become Combat Controllers take a different path, in a fifteen-week course taught at Keesler Air Force Base in Mississippi. There they begin by learning every facet of aircraft control from the ground up (literally), including flight rules and patterns (such as right-hand or left-hand approach), navigational tools such as flares, smoke, rotating beacons, tiny little strobe lights powered by a 9-volt battery that can be seen for twenty miles, weather forecasting (still an imprecise science, but getting better all the time), and how to land and organize a busy military airfield on what might previously have been a farm. They'll fight and take an airfield if one can be found, but a good meadow will do in a pinch. A training period in modern combat techniques is next, with much fieldwork so that they can work easily with Green Berets, Rangers, SEALs, or Marines if the challenge comes up. The final part is their integration into an Air Commando team where CCTs and PJs work together, landing in any one of a number of ways to perform any number of missions.

It is these teams that make up AFSOC today—men who can run CSAR and combat equally well, designate targets with lasers for the "fast movers," control and lead to the ground safely any plane in the Air Force inventory, and also live off the land and fight together with other Special Operations Forces as a seamless component second to none. For this reason they still favor the motto first bestowed on them in World War II: "Anywhere, anytime."

An Air Force SpecOps Combat Controller is awarded a Purple Heart by Lieutenant General Maxwell C. Bailey, commander of AF Special Operations Command. The operator, along with five other CCTs, was wounded near Mazar-i-Sharif, Afghanistan during Operation Enduring Freedom. (U.S. Air Force)

U.S. Army Special Forces— The Green Berets

*I*n the world of Special Operations Forces, one name continues to resonate throughout the world, feared by America's foes and equally welcomed by her allies. More than the British SAS, Soviet Spetsnaz, Mosby's Rangers, or the guys who packed themselves into the Trojan Horse, it is the U.S. Army's Special Forces—or as they are better known from Jakarta to Cairo, the Green Berets— who best symbolize excellence in unconventional warfare.

Surprisingly, however, they are not always understood, even by the American public whom they defend. Blame it on John Wayne. Many people see them as commandos (which can be true enough); or as an aggressive strike force implementing U.S. will around the globe (actually, if tasked with that mission they might pull it off). In reality, Army Special Forces specializes in "force multiplying" American power across the globe, in nations that need our help or our assistance. They make the connections with our natural allies that allow other countries to join the American pursuit of freedom.

Using brains as much as brawn, favoring versatility over brute power, they are the "quiet professionals" who project American values—not through talk but with skills, dedication, diplomacy, and example. Of course, when it comes to combat they are unsurpassed; but that is not their primary mission. Special Forces vets don't go on to become pro wrestlers, though they might end up teaching college. They might lose all their arm-wrestling matches to football lineman, though endurance contests would be another matter. Army Special Forces are not only fighters but leaders; not just commandos but teachers. When operating behind enemy lines, speaking native languages, providing aid or guidance from all perspectives of the military sphere (and also civic action to simply help communities help themselves), they enhance American influence far beyond their own numbers. Among Special Operations Forces, there are enough units dedicated to warfighting and they look the part. A member of Army Special Forces could meanwhile stand next to you at a bus stop and you wouldn't know it. Their primary mission is to project know-how more than force, and in all cases to expand not only America's interests but its values.

History

Army Special Forces will forever be connected with President John F. Kennedy, who prior to his assassination launched them onto the world stage. Unlike the Navy SEALs and Air Force SpecOps, which stem directly from the Frogmen and Air Commandos of World War II, the Green Berets are a creation of the Cold War. Nevertheless, World War II planted two important seeds that would later produce a hybrid fruit when Army Special Forces was created in 1952. Not surprisingly, these were two entirely different kinds of outfits: one with brawn and one with brains.

The first progenitor was the First Special Service Force (FSSF), a joint U.S.–Canadian brigade created in July 1942. Stories persist that the eight hundred Canadian volunteers were excellent, disciplined soldiers while the 1,000-some American volunteers were largely the result of other commanders emptying out their brigs, or getting rid of malcontents. Sort of like the Dirty Dozen writ large. In any case, the formation of the unit spelled bad news for the Germans. Training in Montana, the men practiced close-quarters combat, infiltration, skiing, and mountaineering, as well as airborne and amphibious assaults, and weapons and demolition skills. They adopted the crossed arrows of the 19th-century U.S. Scouts as their insignia.

Their first mission was to invade the island of Kiska in the Aleutians but the Japanese had wisely evacuated the place before their arrival. The British had a notion to use the FSSF as a deep-penetration force in Norway but they were instead sucked into Italy where the Anglo-Americans armies were struggling on their only hot front against the Germans. Arriving in early December 1943, the FSSF was attached to the 36th "Texas" Division, which was then trying to fight its way north toward eventual decimation beneath Monte Cassino. The men of the FSSF were promptly ordered to take two German-held peaks, one featuring a sheer, 200-foot cliff. They accomplished both tasks at the cost of some five hundred casualties. The problem was that once they had proven their skills and courage, 5th Army Command didn't run out of mountains. Ordered to fight its way up another succession of heights against tenacious German paratroopers and grenadiers, the FSSF bled itself white. By the end of its first month in combat the unit had lost fourteen hundred of its original eighteen hundred men.

The unit was transferred to the Anzio bridgehead in February 1944, just after the destruction of Darby's Rangers. (Some of Darby's survivors joined the FSSF.) Holding a division-sized sector of the line by themselves, the First Special Services Force earned a new nickname, "The Devil's Brigade." It came from the diary of a dead German officer who had written, "The black devils are all around us every time we come into line and we never hear them." The Germans were especially spooked at finding some of their comrades each morning with throats slit and crossed-arrow stickers plastered on their foreheads.

During the invasion of southern France, the Devil's Brigade attacked and seized two enemy-held islands flanking the beach-head—a task that required both amphibious and cliff-scaling skills. Inland, they fought through the Vosges Mountains, but by then were resembling line infantry as much as a special force. On December 5, 1944, the Devil's Brigade was disbanded, largely because Canada, whose men had fought like lions from the start of the war, finally issued restrictions on the use of its troops in combat. The brigade, with a nominal strength of 1,825 men, had suffered 2,334 casualties in a year of fighting.

If the First Special Service Force can be considered the blue-collar father of U.S. Special Forces, the mother—whom today's Green Berets more closely resemble—was an entirely different kind of outfit: the Office of Strategic Services, or OSS.

Created during World War II, the OSS had both an intelli-gence function—classic spying and espionage—and a paramili-tary one. The latter was modeled on the activities of Britain's Special Operations Executive and involved infiltrating teams behind German lines to organize, train, and assist local resistance forces.

The operators were organized into Jedburgh teams (named after an area where medieval Scots had resisted English rule), consisting of an American officer, a native officer, and an enlisted radioman. The teams would parachute into the continent at night and make contact with local partisans or Maquis. The teams would call in resupply as necessary (a handy way to gain authority over the locals) and direct operations against German communications, outposts, and depots.

It was extremely hazardous work, not just because the Germans could summon strength in their rear areas to annihilate any resistance group they could find, but because plainclothes operatives were executed if captured. In one incident, an OSS raiding party of fifteen men destroyed an important railway tunnel in Italy but then were trapped on the coast while waiting for extraction. The PT boat sent to pick them up was beaten off by enemy fire and the captured raiders were executed with their hands bound.

In Europe it all came down to D-day and by then the French resistance, aided by American and British operators, was fully in sync with the plan. Roads, rails, and bridges were blown while German manpower was tied down in firefights across the countryside. The greatest concrete achievement of this unconventional war came when the 2nd SS Panzer Division, "Das Reich," which had been resting at full strength inland, was decimated by repeated ambushes and delayed from reaching the invasion front. It was even ordered to pause in central France until the partisans were quelled. (The worst atrocity in the West, at Oradour-sur-Glane, was a result of their frustration.) By the time Das Reich reached Normandy, Allied conventional forces were firmly on shore and the panzer division was destroyed in the subsequent battles.

In the Pacific, MacArthur held tight to his imperatives and refused to allow OSS operations in his bailiwick. In Burma, "Vinegar Joe" Stillwell was also reluctant, but nevertheless allowed an OSS unit called Detachment 101 to operate in his theater. Stillwell soon came to appreciate its efforts and results. Behind-the-lines teams found fertile ground in Southeast Asian populations eager to overthrow Japanese rule. One such "freedom fighter" who coordinated with the OSS was Ho Chi Minh, a leader in the Vietnamese resistance. Just as Osama bin Laden was a pal to the U.S. when he fought against the Soviets in Afghanistan, so was Ho Chi Minh an ally against the Japanese. (U.S. scientists are probably already working on a crystal ball to avoid these kind of embarrassments in the future.)

The OSS lost its great patron when President Roosevelt died in April 1945, and after the war it was disbanded. Many of its personnel joined the CIA, which was formed in 1947, some switched to civilian life, while others went back to the army. The only vestige of special operations now remaining in the army was an Office of Psychological Warfare, because it sounded like a modern sort of concept. In that office was Colonel Aaron Bank, a former Jedburgh, and Colonel Russell Volckmann, who had organized guerrillas against the Japanese in the Philippines while waiting for MacArthur to return. These visionary men outlined the concept of special forces—versatile, multi-skilled soldiers who could exponentially increase U.S. power by coordinating with America's natural allies, operating if need be behind enemy lines.

In December 1951 the army went along with their idea and on June 19, 1952—the 10th anniversary of the birth of the 1st Ranger Battalion—the 10th Special Forces Group was activated. (It was originally given the lineage of the Rangers as well as the First Special Service Force; the Ranger colors and name were later transferred to the LRRPs in Vietnam.)

Though the Korean War was still in full blast, the conflict had already begun to calcify and proved to be a poor environment for special operations anyway. The Special Forces were created more for the possibility of a new, larger war in Europe. They could perform reconnaissance or direct action missions like the Devil's Brigade of yore, but their primary model was the force-multiplying Jedburghs of the OSS. As the scenario went, if the Red Army invaded Western Europe it would immediately find dozens of U.S. Special Forces groups in its rear, mobilizing partisans and targeting communications. The original concept was that Special Forces would be half manned by native Europeans, immigrants who under the Lodge Bill could become American citizens if they served in the military. Fiercely anti-Communist Poles, Czechs, Germans, Hungarians, and others were recruited.

The basic Special Forces unit was an Operational Detachment Alpha— an A-team or ODA—of two officers and ten men. OD-Bravo would coordinate six A-teams and OD-Charlie commanded the Group. Colonel Bank insisted on a rigorous, thorough training regimen, meaning all combat skills and both airborne and amphibious capability. Since Special Forces would work with indigenous peoples, every man had to be fluent in at least two languages. An A-team was designed to bisect if it had to, and all specialized skills, for example radio operation, were duplicated within the team. In practice, every member had a working knowledge of everyone else's job.

In 1953, half of the the 10th Special Forces Group was moved to Germany and the other half was redesignated the 77th SFG based at Smoke Bomb Hill at Fort Bragg. Beginning in 1956, the 77th was requested to form several Special Forces Operational Detachments, to be sent to the Far East. The following year these were consolidated into a new 1st Special Forces Group based on Okinawa.

While tensions alternately rose and fell in Europe, more immediate problems were appearing in Asia where the French, apparently unsatisfied with their humiliation in World War II, were coming up with fresh ones in Indochina. In 1954, Vietnam was split into two after the Communists destroyed a French army at Dien Bien Phu in the north. The real hotspot, however, looked to be Laos, where a royal government was barely holding on against another Red Chinese-backed insurgent movement, the Pathet Lao. In 1959, American Special Forces secretly arrived in the country to form mobile training teams—operations dubbed White Star—to help the Laotian army and native tribesmen battle the Communists.

Though it had grown to three groups deployed on three continents, it cannot be said that Special Forces flourished in the 1950s. For career officers it was more a dead end as the conventional army still dominated councils. All this changed when Dwight Eisenhower was replaced as president by John F. Kennedy, who was committed to military innovation and the idea of elite special forces.

Kennedy, a dashing young president, may have been attracted to special operations due to a personal affinity for small-unit elites and the glamor that attended their exploits. But he also differed with President Eisenhower in his geostrategic worldview. He believed that conventional wars with the Communist world were no longer likely and that the new problem would be guerrilla wars, which already seemed to be popping up across the globe, backed by Soviet or Chinese arms.

After its inception, Army Special Forces troops had begun to wear green berets to symbolize their commitment and to express a certain spirit in their oft-neglected unit. They wore the beret in the field but the army brass refused to let them wear it on base. The army wanted nothing to do with "special" soldiers who had their own ideas of how to dress. In his first year as president, Kennedy visited Fort Bragg and made it clear that the Special

Forces—and their headgear—fit in perfectly with his concept of what the United States needed to meet its future challenges. He called the green beret "a symbol of excellence, a badge of courage, a mark of distinction in the fight for freedom." Addressing Congress, he stated his intention to substantially expand "the orientation of existing forces for the conduct of non-nuclear war, paramilitary operations and sub-limited, or unconventional wars." The public supported his vision and was excited by the idea of these elite new Special Forces, whom everyone now called the "Green Berets."

During Kennedy's short tenure, four new Special Forces Groups were created—the 3rd, 5th, 6th, and 8th (the 77th was redesignated the 7th)—and members of Special Forces were added to the Reserve and National Guard. Laos, a landlocked country bordering North Vietnam, soon began to look like a losing investment and strategically marginal besides. But South Vietnam was having serious trouble resisting its own insurgency. In September 1961, the 5th Special Forces Group was assigned to that country. In practice, for the next decade, nearly all Special Forces personnel would funnel for a spell through the 5th's command.

The first problem encountered by the Green Berets in Vietnam was that they had hoped to find a potentially dedicated, skilled force of native Vietnamese guerrillas willing to resist a foreign army. They did, but unfortunately it was fighting for the other side. The Special Forces soon realized that their task would not be to organize an insurgency but rather a counterinsurgency, because the Americans, as often as not, were viewed as the occupying power (or as many peasants thought, "new French").

The Special Forces's motto, "de oppresso liber"—"to free the oppressed"—bears a certain poignancy in regard to Vietnam, in that the Green Berets, inspired by Kennedy's rousing calls to pay

Green Berets in action in Vietnam. A medic provides aid to a wounded officer while another trooper, holding a grenade, counterattacks over the hill against a North Vietnamese assault. (AP)

any price for freedom, dived into that morass with all the best intentions. It had simply never occurred to the Special Forces, or to the U.S. public, that a population under attack by Communist troops would consider Americans, of all people, the bad guys. (If it's any comfort, the Soviet Union later experienced that same kind of shock in Afghanistan.)

In Vietnam, while it still seemed a doable project, the Green Berets got to work organizing and training the indigenous peoples to defend themselves. The concept was to form Civilian Irregular Defense Groups (CIDGs) in remote border areas where the Viet Cong and, beginning in 1965, the North Vietnamese Army, operated with impunity. The natives were often Meo or Montagnard tribesmen (disliked by other Vietnamese, North and South) or Nung, Chinese ethnics, many of them refugees from Mao Tse Tung. The Green Berets built forts to protect the hamlets while applying their other skills to help the locals with medical care, infrastructure, or communications. The CIDG units were designed as an interlocking network so that one could come to the help of another if attacked. The Special Forces also created mobile strike forces (Mikes) that could not only respond to crises but take the war to the enemy. If the Communists employed guerrilla tactics, so could the Green Berets strike back against VC or NVA columns or base camps.

The success of the CIDG concept caused it to be altered by the high command in Saigon, to the program's detriment. The army decided that the Special Forces camps should be placed in the most remote, dangerous parts of the country to block Communist movement and supply. Thus, instead of securing large segments of the countryside, the camps became isolated Fort Apaches near the border, under near constant attack.

In July 1964, the Green Beret/CIDG camp at Nam Dong was nearly overrun by a Viet Cong battalion. During the five-hour fight, Green Beret Captain Roger Donlon, wounded twice, rallied the defenders and became the war's first recipient of the Medal of Honor.

In 1965, North Vietnamese assaults on the camp at Plei Mei triggered the Battle of the Ia Drang Valley, the first major clash between American and NVA regulars. In 1966, a Special Forces compound at A Shau was simply overrun by VC and NVA attacking in human waves. Too many parts of the perimeter

Special Forces soldiers explore the entire gamut of SpecOps warfare, as seen here on a training mission with SCUBA. (U.S. Army)

caved in. This one turned ugly and when Medevacs came in to take out wounded, Green Berets had to fire on their own panicked CIDGs to keep them from swamping the helicopters. A column was formed to retreat through the jungle, but again, when Medevacs swooped down, the U.S. and loyal ARVNs had to beat back their native allies to let the wounded be put aboard.

In May 1967 the camp at Lang Vei, in the northwest corner of South Vietnam, was abandoned after being penetrated by NVA troops. They reached the command bunker and killed both officers of the A-team. The site was valuable as flank defense for Khe Sanh, however, and a new fort was built on more defensible ground one thousand yards away.

The most famous disaster came at Lang Vei in February 1968, when the new compound was overrun by Communist tanks. Lang Vei was barely a mile from the Laotian border and within artillery range of Khe Sanh, where a large force of Marines was then surrounded by three NVA divisions. At Lang Vei, the Americans knew enemy tanks were in the area so they had acquired a quantity of LAWs (Light Anti-Tank Weapons). But their reports were not believed elsewhere and the Green Berets themselves thought the NVA would use their tanks as mobile artillery. Instead, on the night of February 6, the Communist armor attacked along with their infantry, charging head-on. NVA sappers preceded the armor, cutting the wires and dismantling mines. Once the tanks were inside, almost the entire CIDG contingent, along with many Laotian troops who had come into the compound for safety, panicked. Green Beret Lieutenant Colonel Daniel Schungel organized two-man hunter-killer teams to destroy the tanks, but most of their LAWs didn't work. They either misfired or bounced off the armor. The Americans and some remaining South Vietnamese took to assaulting the tanks with phosphorous grenades, recoilless rifles, or any weapon available, including bare hands to pry open the hatches. Seven tanks were knocked out. The Marines at Khe Sanh helped with artillery fire, but just as at A Shau, were not overly quick to come to the Special Forces's assistance. The camp was destroyed and thence abandoned, as was Khe Sanh a few months later.

In Vietnam, the Special Forces's concept of force multiplication, enabling native troops to fight their own wars, ran smack into the rest of the military's concept, beginning in 1965, to combat the enemy themselves. That year, the bestselling song in the country was "The Ballad of the Green Berets," written and sung by one of their own. A few years later, the John Wayne movie, "The Green Berets," played nationwide. These events did not really help the Special Forces once the Marines, army infantry, armor, air force, and everyone else was in the war.

The Special Forces had meanwhile run short of men, and whereas before Vietnam only 10 percent of volunteers had passed the training cycle, now 70 percent were doing so, despite the fact that the Special Forces were now taking civilians. Some of these men who volunteered for the thickest of combat were not necessarily well-rounded individuals. The rest of the army had a name for them: "Snake eaters," and the Special Forces were gradually coming to resemble one of their forebears, the Devil's Brigade. Things worsened when Special Forces became the primary manpower resource for SOG, the prosaically named Studies and Observation Group. (It was really a Special Operations Group, designed for cross-border raids and recon into North Vietnam, Laos, and Cambodia.) SOG placed the Green Berets farther outside the normal chain of command, or any previous army concept of unit discipline. Special Forces also began to work closely with the CIA, its sister progeny from the OSS. The Green Berets, in their remote outposts, surrounded by natives, disdaining army discipline, and up to who knows what, began to be resented by the regular citizen soldiers who were acquiring enough combat experience of their own.

The Green Berets in Vietnam came to an ignominious end after some officers executed a Vietnamese double-agent on the advice of the CIA. General Creighton Abrams, who had commanded armor in World War II, took the opportunity to evict the

5th Special Forces Group from the country. In the trial that followed, President Nixon ordered the CIA not to testify because the entire affair involved the then-clandestine bombing of NVA sanctuaries in Cambodia. Though charges were dropped, the affair left a stain on the Green Berets's reputation. It was a cruel coda for what had been the most decorated unit in the war, with 17 Medals of Honor, 60 Distinguished Service Crosses, 814 Silver Stars, and 13,234 Bronze Stars. The 5th Special Forces Group, never numbering over 2,400 men, came out of the war with 2,658 Purple Hearts.

By March 1971, the Special Forces—who no longer wished to be called Green Berets—were gone from Vietnam and their guidance of native troops near the Cambodian and Laotian borders was handed over to the South Vietnamese. Ironically, this move was portrayed as part of America's new "Vietnamization" policy (the official code name for retreat) though the Special Forces had been practicing Vietnamization all along. Each A-team of twelve men had directed, defended, advised, and supplied an average of some five hundred native fighters, far away from the major cities and between the jaws of main-force Communist units. Once U.S. conventional forces had withdrawn, the North Vietnamese attacked straight through the Central Highlands, where the Special Forces A-teams, with Montagnard, Meo, and South Vietnamese defenders, had previously challenged them to go. In 1975 the country collapsed in about five weeks. It would have fallen sooner except NVA columns found the roads too crammed with refugees.

After Vietnam, both morale and public support for the U.S. military fell into a downward spiral and the Special Forces worried about their survival within the army. Nixon was thrown out of office after one too many cover-ups and then President Ford was replaced by the liberal-minded Jimmy Carter. Hollywood didn't help with its big-budget "Apocalypse Now," an impressionistic movie depiction of the Vietnam War. It concerned a colonel at the head of a private army deep within Indochina, his men ranging from hollow-eyed U.S. soldiers to bones-in-the-nose mountain tribesmen. His moral compass had gone off the rails and another U.S. officer had been dispatched to eliminate him.

As the 1970s progressed, Army Special Forces devised an operation called SPARTAN (Special Proficiency at Rugged Training and Nation Building). It tasked A-teams with going around the United States, to depressed rural areas or Indian reservations to help build local infrastructure—roads, bridges, schools—and to provide medical care and engineering and civic expertise. As the "Me" decade ran its course, Army Special Forces devoted its incredible range of skills to helping people help themselves, pitching in with sweat and dedication to raise the standard of living of America's economically oppressed. This is not to say, however, that the Special Forces were not looking forward to the end of the "national malaise," when they would once again be called upon for their most unique skills.

This would happen after 1980's Desert One fiasco in Iran. It was suddenly realized that America had let its Special Operations capacity slip away. Further, with the rise of radical Islam in addition to the nonstop proliferation of Communist insurgencies in Latin America, Africa, and elsewhere, American influence had obviously declined. The humanistic intellectual, Jimmy Carter, a president who carried his own bags, was replaced in 1981 by an ex-movie star from California who preferred to ride in limos, Ronald Reagan. In 1982, Army Special Forces tightened its recruiting standards and lengthened its training process. In 1983, Special Forces didn't participate in the slam-bang, thinly disguised SNAFU of Grenada, but now a lot of good men were coming into the army and trying to make Special Forces.

As America began to feel its oats again in the 1980s, Special Forces served as the vanguard in projecting U.S. military doctrine and training throughout the world. The task was termed Foreign Internal Defense (FID) and meant that if a country opted for the American rather than the Soviet camp, Special Forces would arrive to train its troops and provide a connection to U.S. weaponry, resources, and philosophy. In the mid-1980s, Latin America boiled with Communist guerrillas backed by Cuba and the Soviets. Special Forces dispatched to El Salvador and Honduras helped ensure that the war in Nicaragua was contained, until the Nicaraguan Sandanistas were finally, grudgingly, overthrown in free elections.

In December 1989, Special Forces played a key role in the invasion of Panama. Dropped into the interior by helicopter, they destroyed one of Manuel Noriega's radio transmitting stations. In another action, an A-team and a half (18 men) were flown in to hold a bridge against a vehicle column of Panamanian reinforcements. Once the fighting had ended, Spanish-speaking A-teams spread throughout the countryside calming the populace and accepting surrenders. (Nearly all of these were eagerly offered.)

The following year, America had a major war on its hands after Iraq's invasion of Kuwait. General H. Norman Schwarzkopf, commander of the American-led coalition, had held a grudge against Special Forces since his days as an infantry officer in Vietnam. But he soon found out that he needed them. The great coalition was a veritable babel of different languages, doctrine, weapons, and training levels. Teams from the 10th Special Forces Group, Europe, came down to coordinate those contingents while the Arabic-speaking 5th SFG spread among the Muslim forces. A total of 109 foreign battalions gained Special Forces advisers to integrate them into the campaign and, once the offensive began, accompany them into battle. The Special Forces's most noteworthy achievement during this phase was recreating the Kuwaiti army from troops who had fled the initial invasion and from civilian refugees. When coalition forces rolled in to liberate Kuwait City, they were led by Kuwaiti army columns, the men of the 5th SFG trying to remain discreetly to the side.

During the defensive stage of the campaign, Desert Shield, Schwarzkopf had turned down offers by Special Forces to penetrate Iraq. But once the Desert Storm air campaign kicked off, teams were inserted into the country to track enemy troop movements and to hunt Scud missiles. In one incident, an A-team was dropped north of the Euphrates River and quickly built a hidesite by an irrigation canal. At daybreak the men were dismayed to find Iraqi children playing around their position. Suddenly the scampering kids went quiet, and then they ran. The hide-site had been compromised. A few of the sniper-trained Special Forces jumped up with rifles but there was no way they were going to fire. The team began moving to a new position as an Iraqi column came down the road and began disgorging troops. The A-team called for air support as it engaged 150 Iraqi troops in a firefight. At one point the enemy began creeping down the irrigation canal, but the Special Forces team leader counterattacked, killing their lead men and forcing the rest to run. For the rest of the day, the A-team held off attacks while F-16s swooped down to keep Iraqi reinforcements at bay. That night, two Night Stalker Black Hawks arrived, almost landing on the A-team's heads, to perform the extraction.

During the 1990s, Special Forces were at the forefront of U.S. participation in the coalitions in Bosnia and Kosovo, while the 7th SFG was tasked with operations in Haiti. There the A-teams engaged in a series of Civil Actions rather than Direct Action combat.

Just weeks after September 11, 2001, the American public

When all else fails, send in the cavalry. In November 2001, the U.S. public was tickled by pictures showing Army Special Forces operators riding horseback across Afghanistan with troops from the Northern Alliance. (Dept. of Defense)

learned that U.S. Army personnel were already on the ground in Afghanistan. These were Special Forces A-teams covertly inserted to liaison with anti-Taliban Afghans. The A-teams engaged in a number of firefights and coordinated U.S. air support to even the odds against Taliban counterattacks. Interestingly, much of the U.S. public had never heard of these "A-teams," who now seemed to be America's best foot forward in a war fought with the greatest reservoir of moral authority since World War II. It was left to news reporters to explain that these mysterious A-teams, or A-detachments, were the men once known as the Green Berets. And at the beginning of the 21st century their motto had not changed: "de oppresso liber."

In January 2002, an A-team assisted in the assault on a Kandahar hospital held by Taliban diehards. After the Taliban had been eliminated, a Special Forces operator provided a report on his radio while an Afghan looked on. (AP)

Training

Special Forces draws its recruits from throughout the army, favoring mature soldiers, proficient at their specialty. Though many Special Operations units (particularly Air Force) like to see brains as well as brawn in their ranks, Army Special Forces prioritizes it. Of course recruits have to be fine athletes: strong, agile, with incredible endurance, and also good shots. But in addition they need a second (or third) language, diplomatic, teaching, and negotiation skills and—most valuable of all—a talent for decisive leadership within the mission imperative. In the business world, they call this a "self-starter."

Special Forces runs a department called "Selection and

Mountain warfare has been part of Special Forces training for decades. These skills were put to good use during the 2001-02 war in Afghanistan. (U.S. Army)

A sergeant of the 10th Special Forces Group (right) instructs two Navy Seabees on mortar tactics during a 1997 exercise in Colorado. A primary mission of the Green Berets is to convey their skills to other units, whether American or allied. (Dept. of Defense.)

Assessment" that puts volunteers through twenty-four days of psychological and physical tests to see who can be admitted to the real training process. If they're over twenty-two and a sergeant, or on the list to be one (in the case of officers, a captain or a promotable lieutenant) they'll give them a look. If they're not yet airborne-qualified, they need to prepare to be so. Those who get through the initial assessment will then be put through months of the most arduous training that generations of instructors have been able to devise. One can quit at any time and say, "OK, I've seen what it's like, get me back to my unit." Or if they get injured they can be put on standby with a chance to try again. Incredibly enough, some guys make it through the physical, technical, and mental travails.

But over 90 percent of applicants fail to make Special Forces; still, as in all walks of life, certain skills or characteristics can give you an edge. Soldiers who are a whiz in their specialties, say combat medicine, may find that Special Forces has a need for those skills at the time. In addition, fluent language skills or ethnicity are a plus. The latter is not from political correctness but because Special Forces works among foreign populations and militaries.

After Selection and Assessment, the survivors enter the Qualification course, which is divided into three parts. The first, lasting forty days, is basic skills, including reconnaissance, navigation, marksmanship, and fieldcraft. The second divides candidates by their specialties—team leadership, weapons, engineering, intelligence, communications, medical—and involves courses at various schools together lasting half a year. The third phase is when everyone comes together for forty days of unit training, performing as an A-team. By this time candidates are fully qualified to serve with almost every other elite unit in the world. But Special Forces has a final, and crucial, stage of selection. It's called Robin Sage and takes place in the countryside of North Carolina.

This elaborate test hypothesizes the state of Pineland, representing a foreign country occupied by an enemy power. Within Pineland are enemy soldiers (OpForce) and potentially friendly guerillas (G's), both groups played by Special Forces members or veterans. A unique touch is that many North Carolinians, spread across five counties (4,500 square miles) also play along with the exercise, providing succor, intelligence, and safe houses. Recruits must be cautious, however, because civilians could also be working for OpForce. Robin Sage has been taking place for nearly fifty years so many of the real civilians have been participating for generations.

The trainees, now formed into A-teams, are infiltrated into Pineland and given specific missions, changed with each exercise so recruits won't know what to expect. One of the fundamental tasks is to make contact with the G's and gain their assistance. The non-coms playing the G's don't make it easy, pretending to be stubborn or hostile until the newcomers gain their trust. At the end of the two-week exercise, the candidate A-team is tasked with seizing an OpForce objective. All the while, Special Forces instructors assess the recruits in all facets of their performance.

In February 2002, a tragedy occurred in Pineland when two Special Forces trainees were shot by a law enforcement officer, one killed and one wounded. The lawman stopped two men in a pick-up truck and noticed a dismantled M-4 carbine in a bag. He didn't realize they were really Special Forces prospects; the trainees didn't realize that the nervous officer wasn't a part of the scenario and was preparing to wield lethal force. After this incident, Special Forces tightened up their controls on the exercise so that civilians, trainees, and local sheriff's departments are all on the same page.

If one makes it into Special Forces the next job—ironically enough for the "quiet professionals"—is to intensify their foreign language skills. And for many personnel, political and military history courses, diplomatic, geographical, or anthropological studies are pursued between deployments and continued training. Many soldiers obsessively follow world news—after all, during a career in Army Special Forces there's an excellent chance they'll be a part of it.

CHAPTER 6

Delta
Force

*D*elta Force, the most recent addition to the United States Special Forces arsenal, is the direct outgrowth of one man and his experience with the fabled British Special Air Service (SAS). When Green Beret Colonel Charles A. ("Chargin' Charlie") Beckwith went on an exchange with the SAS in 1963, including hazardous service in Malaysia, he came back with more than just a taste for tea. In his time with the elite British force, Beckwith saw a way that the United States could go beyond the standard of "special" units to create its own version of the SAS with all that implied, such as complete autonomy, a free hand in selection of gear and tactics, and a veil that covered its actions to deny knowledge about the unit to any potential enemy. To this day it is very hard to gain authoritative insight into Delta Force and its doings, and that's how they like it. What is known is that Delta is the premier military counterterrorism force in the United States, and does its work with a surprising lack of notice from the press or public. Based at Fort Bragg, North Carolina (convenient to their Airborne and Green Beret colleagues), behind an imposing series of gates and fences, the men of Delta accomplish much while revealing little.

History

Beckwith's notion of an American SAS had to wait for more than ten years to come to fruition, due to reluctance on the part of the U.S. Army to expand Special Forces beyond the units already on hand. But in November of 1977 the first Delta troopers started operations without fanfare under the name 1st Special Forces Operational Detachment Delta. It meant an entirely new concept for the U.S. Army Special Forces. (The word "Delta" was used as next in line, because Special Forces already consisted of Alpha, Bravo, and Charlie detachments.) But creating a new unit had required both budgetary infighting as well as turf battles within the army community. While some American military thinkers and planners had watched the British SAS and German GSG-9 counterterrorist units as they ramped up during the 1970s taking an active role against the wave of terrorist acts that beset that decade, units like the Rangers and Green Berets had no interest in losing recruits to some fancy new secret organization. After all, they already had elite troops and provision for fast reaction; what more was needed? Surely nobody wanted another box in the table of organization. Only a hard core of supporters and advocates continued to press for Delta to get a chance to show what it could do.

One of the oddities of Delta is that its troops are expected to be able to go anywhere and blend into any population, meaning that such time-honored military features as a "tactical" haircut (which translates into a severe buzz that is "high speed/low drag") would be discouraged. They might wear civilian clothing just as much as battle dress uniforms (BDUs), and might test and train with exotic weapons and gear. This kind of maverick sensibility, already much in evidence among Navy SEALs, is a sure way to anger traditional military leadership. One way or another the Delta troops heard every variation of the standard objections to all Special Forces: you dress oddly, do things your own way, have an ease and familiarity between officers and NCOs that is non-regulation, take all the best troops, use weird gear, and seem to come and go as you please. It was optimistic to expect this style of counterterrorist warfare to find supporters in an organization as large and traditional as the U.S. Army.

Missions

In 1979 the call came for a joint task force that could resolve the six-month captivity of fifty-three Americans held hostage in Iran by Ayatollah Khomeni's radical Muslims in Tehran. President Jimmy Carter had tried every avenue to try to resolve the hostage issue, and in a desperate move decided to launch a commando operation that would free the Americans from the midst of a hostile capital. Special Forces veterans such as Dick Meadows, who was a civilian advisor to Delta after a long career filled with dangerous missions in Vietnam and elsewhere, were brought onboard when the CIA proved unable to provide good human intelligence on the ground. Meadows was given a cover as an Irish national, and began preparing the way for a mixed force of army, navy, Marine, and air force special operators. Meanwhile a group of 132 men, a mixture of Delta, Ranger, and Special Forces, were to be flown to Germany and then Egypt before winging their way to Desert One, the remote site where they would link up with helicopters, which were coming in from the aircraft carrier *Nimitz*. The plan was for the rescue force to link up with their choppers and then go to Desert Two southeast of the city, where trucks were waiting. Then, after a final reconnaissance, the force would drive into Tehran and hit the three places where the hostages were being held, while AC-130 Spectre gunships would orbit overhead to not only hammer the two Iranian jets that were in readiness at the airport, but also use their gatling guns and howitzers to hose down any crowds that threatened the rescue.

But Delta's first operation was complicated in its conception and finally went up in flames when a helicopter collided with a fuel-laden airplane at Desert One, producing a fireball that ended the mission. Two of the eight helicopters from the *Nimitz* had failed to arrive, and another had malfunctioned in the desert. The mission had been aborted even before the tragic accident, since the U.S. had come up one helicopter short of the six necessary for the mission. As Delta and the rest of the team flew back to Egypt, Dick Meadows was able to go to the airport and take a flight out. Despite their best efforts, Delta's initial entry into the world of Special Operations was a non-starter. Interestingly, there was no mention of Delta in the media; all that came out was that American commandos had tried and failed to rescue the hostages.

A second rescue attempt (codenamed "Honey Badger") was put in the works, but was cancelled when the American captives were freed following Jimmy Carter's departure from office. Delta had nevertheless secured a place in the pantheon of Special Operations by virtue of its capabilities, and now expanded from one hundred to three hundred men, or three troops of three squadrons each. With a radical revolution and the threat of American hostages taking place on the Caribbean island of Grenada in 1983, Delta was called upon to land ahead of the majority of American forces, and for the first time they used their aviation assets, the 160th SOAR (Special Operations Aviation Regiment), known as the "Night Stalkers." In advance of the Ranger force that was to parachute onto the airfield at Point Salines, Delta was ferried ashore by their helicopters and assaulted the control tower at the airfield. They also attacked the prison at Richmond Hill, where they lost a Black Hawk to antiaircraft fire. One outcome of Grenada was that for the first time, both the 160th SOAR as well as Delta were covered by news organizations. But the lid came off in those years in some other ways as well, because a few unscrupulous Delta Force members used tricky accounting to cook their books and abscond with funds. And while the cases were handled quietly, the press picked up on some of that as well.

The 1980s saw Delta deployed to a bewildering array of foreign locales, often having their missions called off, but always marching to the sound of the guns and gaining experience, as well as important contacts with Special Operations Forces around the world. In Italy, Germany, Lebanon, the Philippines, Central and South America, Delta responded to most of the major hijackings and hostage rescues of those anarchic years. Unfortunately, they were often called off by higher authorities for a variety of reasons, and they deeply resented the interference. But being good soldiers, they always followed orders. In war-torn Beirut they prowled through alleys and hunted for Americans held hostage, including CIA station chief William Buckley and Marine Corps officer William Higgins, both of whom were tortured to death by their captors. Delta also had a hand in thwarting a number of aircraft hijackings, including at least one where they found themselves surrounded by Italian troops bent on maintaining their jurisdiction despite the presence of the elite Americans.

Also, in operations that spurred discussion of the use of U.S. forces in their own country, Delta provided security detachments for the Olympics in Los Angeles and the centennial of the Statue of Liberty in 1986. After the Los Angeles deployment word was leaked that one of the Delta vehicles was an everyday beer truck,

A rare photo of Delta Force troops in the field, here during 1989's Operation Just Cause in Panama. Delta operators kickstarted the operation by shooting their way through guards to free a U.S. hostage held in a Panama City prison. Normally their operations are kept classified.

guaranteed to attract no attention. Just as in the desert or forest, stealth and mobility depend on blending in, and what could attract less attention than a beer truck at a large sporting event? Though naturally unconfirmable, rumors abound that Delta also has its own aviation resources, disguised as civilian craft.

In 1989 Delta was part of the operation to remove Panamanian leader Manuel Noriega. At H-hour, they started the invasion with the rescue of an American businessman being held hostage in a Panama City prison. Landing on the roof by helicopter, Delta troopers left a security detail there and then stormed into the building, shooting their way through smoke and jail guards, until they found the right cell. Then they blew the door off with enough explosive force to open it, but not so much C-4 as to hurt the businessman. Eliminating everyone who stood in their way, the small team ran for the roof, were able to remount their helicopter and get blocks away before ground fire forced them to land in the street. Most of the operators were injured but still kept to their weapons. Eventually, three American M-113 armored personnel carriers showed up, and the businessman and the Delta troopers were taken to safety. When you look at the MH-6J "Little Bird" helicopter used in this operation, with its external troop seats providing a better than ringside seat of the mayhem on the ground in Panama, and consider the thrill of low-level flight under heavy fire, you have to commend anyone who would consent to travel in such a thing at all, never mind flying into combat to assault a well-guarded jail.

In 1990 Saddam Hussein's forces rolled into Kuwait, fully expecting to make an unopposed grab for oil and power. But President Bush and his British, French, and Saudi allies (eventually joined by most of the world) determined that there would be opposition. During the long protracted build-up of men and material, one of the assets that found its way into Iraq was Delta Force.

Once the punishing air campaign got underway in January 1991, Hussein quickly realized that this was the warm-up for a world-class shellacking. In a desperate attempt to rally the Arab world to his cause, he began launching long-range Scud missiles at Israel, hoping for a violent response that would break up the American-led coalition. Scuds are not known for either reliability or accuracy, but their 2,000-pound warheads can do a lot of damage. As the Israelis threatened to mount their own retaliations against Iraq, it was considered vital in U.S. councils to negate the Scuds before America's pan-global coalition was disrupted by Israeli action. The difficulty was that the missiles were mounted on truck launchers that could be easily hidden and moved about the featureless moonscape of Iraq. The launchers were hard to spot from the air, and hard to hit twenty minutes later by bombers. But in the first use of a technology that has since become a central part of Special Operations Forces repertoire, the launchers could be laser-designated from the ground with a special device onto which jets could then release homing missiles. The British SAS was already Scud-hunting in Iraq but they had taken some losses. Most of the Green Berets in the theater were busy providing guidance to coalition contingents. So Delta was called in for the mission.

Here's where hard training and versatility pay off. It was possible to infiltrate most of the launching areas typically used by the Iraqis either by helicopters or by use of parachutes in either HAHO (high altitude, high opening) or HALO (high altitude, low opening) modes. These are far from standard military jumps, because the altitude where you leave the plane is usually thirty thousand feet, necessitating the use of oxygen in the thin air. Fortunately, Delta is trained for all these methods of insertion, as well as many more. Intelligence reports pinpointed the likely areas, and small teams went in by whatever method was quickest or by the best means possible, usually at night. Due to the high tempo of Special Operations, many of the Black Hawk and Pave Hawk helicopters were already committed to other tasks, but with their HAHO and HALO abilities, infiltration was the least of Delta's worries.

Once on the ground, deep behind enemy lines, Delta teams dug in, using camouflage to make a place where they could hole up for days if necessary. Setting up a discrete satellite link, they were soon settled into their new home and enjoying an MRE

(Meals Ready to Eat) and a swig of precious water. Then they would go out in the night with their second or third generation night vision binoculars and begin to sweep the landscape. On the best missions, a carrier would be spotted or show up after a day or two, and then a world of options opened up to the Delta troopers. They could simply call the coordinates in to the Air Force and wait for a jet to swoop down and cream the Scud, or in the case of darkness or clouds they could use a laser designator to provide the jets with a beam to lock "smart" bombs onto. Or they could use the amazing Barrett "light 50," a .50-caliber, bolt-operated (or semiautomatic in other configurations) rifle, to send their regards from up to a mile away. Any of these methods tended to degrade the Scuds' (or its operators') performance. From the Iraqi perspective, one can only imagine the horror of being eliminated behind one's own lines, or being destroyed as if by a thunderbolt once USAF "fast movers" came over the horizon.

The result was a vastly lessened effectiveness for Saddam Hussein's terror weapons, and the protection of both our troops and the people of Israel. While it was more a combat role for Delta rather than a counterterrorist operation, it was still a finicky job that only the most highly trained and intelligent Special Forces operators could pull off.

A vastly different campaign was waged in the early 1990s in Somalia, and it was there, as part of the famous "person snatch" immortalized in the book and movie "Black Hawk Down," that two Delta sergeants lost their lives, and also won the Medal of Honor. Sergeants Gary I. Gordon and Randall D. Shughart were part of the attempt to snatch the Somali warlord Aidid, in an operation that suffered both from a lack of contingency planning and an underestimation of the difficulties of urban warfare in a land where the populace was both armed and hostile.

On October 3, 1993, a force of Rangers and Delta were

dropped from helicopters onto a slum headquarters where some of Aidid's aides were having a meeting. Delta was assigned to the snatch while the Rangers provided security. An additional force of Rangers drove through the streets in a column of Humvees, the rugged and beefy replacement for the jeep, in order to extract the U.S. troops and their prisoners. But when a helicopter was shot down and there were wounded members of Delta and the 160th SOAR on the ground, the tunes on the dance card changed. Rangers and Delta began converging on the crash site, as a rain of fire came down on their heads. Worst of all, it was every soldier's nightmare: vast crowds of armed Somalis converged on the site, sometimes using women and children as shields while they fired. It would be six hours before the relief column reached the site.

When a second Black Hawk was shot down about a mile away, its pilot, Chief Warrant Officer Michael Durant, thought he had reached the end of the line. And that's when two Delta Force troopers fast-roped from a chopper and came to his aid. They were Sergeants Gordon and Shughart. They had seen the helpless crew trapped in the midst of a hostile crowd blazing away, and they requested three times to be inserted before their commander finally agreed. Once on the ground they fought their way to the downed chopper and set up a perimeter with their own bodies shielding the wounded. The two sergeants killed an undetermined number of Somalis before being killed themselves. It was a heroic action against hopeless odds. Fortunately Durant survived, though he was held prisoner by the Somalis for eleven days before being released. In all, during that terrible day and night, eighteen Americans were killed and eighty-three wounded. It was estimated that three hundred Somalis were killed and another seven hundred wounded by Delta, Rangers, 10th Mountain Division reinforcements, and Night Stalkers during the battle.

The 1990s saw Delta Force honing its skills and learning to deal with an increasingly dangerous world, culminating in the terrorist attacks of September 2001 in New York and Washington. While their training and actions have been cloaked in secrecy, they are known to have been among the first on the ground in Afghanistan, using their skills to pursue America's enemies inside their barren homeland, either bringing them to justice or bringing justice to them.

And the men of Delta still stand ready in the shadows.

Training

Recruiting for Delta Force is a mixture of word of mouth recommendations, volunteers, and even the seemingly prosaic method of an advertisement in *Infantry*, the army's professional magazine. In keeping with Special Forces policy, anyone who is twenty-two years old, a member of the U.S. Army, and can get some recommendations and pass a physical is welcome to apply. Because the job they are being asked to do is a very particular one, involving the use of deadly force in a surgical application and the keeping of a low profile, loudmouths and gorillas won't do. Recruits need to be able to think on their own, and also be team players; to have all the skills and discipline of regular soldiers, and yet be able to think outside the box and transcend some of the training the regular army gives them.

But before they can get to the training phase, they have to go through a month-long selection process, where Delta trainers watch their every move and stand ready to return them to a normal life in a heartbeat. Physical and psychological tests of every sort are thrown at them, and they have to be able to not only meet and exceed expectations, but in some cases not be told what the standards are, adding to the psychological pressures.

One example is the eighteen-mile speed march, for which

135

they are on their own, and not told what time is expected. Informed sources estimate that ten-minute miles are not quite fast enough, which works out to candidates covering eighteen miles in under three hours. In the end, some quit, and some are washed out. Then the survivors are taken to any one of a number of remote and secure locations, whether they be in North Carolina, West Virginia, or Nevada, and that's when the forty-mile land navigation exercise begins.

For this event, carrying a 55-pound rucksack, the prospective troopers are given a spot on the map to reach, perhaps five or six miles away, and told to go as fast as they can. When they get there, the next destination on the map is shown to them, and it's off again. What they do not know is that this will just keep on going and going, sometimes for twelve or fourteen hours at a time, and darkness will fall, and the treacherous terrain will only get more hilly and forested and dark, and yet still on it goes. If they can't keep themselves going from place to place, over forty miles for hour after hour of seemingly aimless wanderings at the whim of someone who picks places that are hard to access, they are probably not Delta material.

By this point, many of those who started the selection process have washed out. If so, they are given a letter saying they have participated in the training, and quietly sent on their way. There's no shame in not having what it takes. But the most feared event is still ahead for those who can also survive the endless PT drill, the driving rain and blazing sun, and the long hours of hard work. They have been pushed physically and psychologically, but now comes the dreaded interview, which is simply sitting down for four hours with a panel of Delta veterans who will ask pointed questions and want to hear the best answers. And the questions are not just about military matters. The panel wants to get an idea about what kind of person they are, not just in a uniform, and to see what other characteristics they exhibit. Only those who can somehow come up with the right things to say and the right responses to questions that often have no answer will be passed. They already know they can shoot and march. The question has become: can they think and express themselves?

By now there are just ten out of every one hundred men left from the original selection process, and that's the way Delta likes it: quality over quantity. They are looking for some of the toughest and smartest warriors on the planet, and it's understandable that barely one in ten would make the grade. The men who make it are now free to go on to the five-month training phase at Fort Bragg, where they will hone their skills at such places as Smoke Bomb Hill and the Killing House. To understand the thrust of this training you have to remember the kinds of jobs that Delta Force will be called on to do: liberating embassies, thwarting hijackers on planes, trains, and ships, acting as bodyguards, and confronting violent and hostile terrorist forces at a moments notice. As a counterterrorist force, Delta is called in when something bad has already happened, and only swift and sure intervention can retrieve the situation. They need to move to the place where the trouble is in a quick and reliable way; make sure someone is collecting intelligence and is able to give them a very thorough rundown on the situation the moment they arrive; set up their headquarters for Command, Control and Communications (C3); make a plan; swarm in and neutralize the opposition while saving the hostages; and then withdraw. And all of it quickly and quietly, except for the part where they shoot all the bad guys twice in the head—the famous "double tap." It's simple enough in outline, but the training takes a while to perfect the procedure with groups of anywhere from four to forty.

Depending on what skills they bring from their previous military training, they can build on those as well as cross-train (as

SEALs and A-teams do) in all the other skills they may need in case a member of their team is put out of action. The most important skills are shooters (both close up and sniping), entry (called "door kicking" although it may also involve lock-picking), explosives (from tiny dabs of C-4 to massive blasts), target identification, communications, and intelligence work.

Because of the jobs at hand, Delta spends many hours every day practicing close quarter combat in a variety of scenarios. This training takes place in as many different settings as the trainers can come up with, including mock-ups of houses and airplanes, and a large number of doors that need to be shot off, kicked down, blown off their hinges, or simply bypassed by means of rappelling through the window. Entry teams may be made up of four people or ten, depending on the size of the room and the number of hostiles inside, but they need to be coordinated so that everyone knows their job and where the other team member's lines of fire are to be expected. They practice again and again to enter quickly, identify the terrorists and the hostages, and shoot or otherwise neutralize the bad guys. Old habits like slow shooting must be broken, and instead replaced with fast and accurate fire on a target as small as an eyeball at fifty feet, and then all the enemies get the double tap. Delta Force shows very little interest in negotiating once they've begun an entry. They may use grenades without shrapnel, called "flashbangs," whose light and noise will disorient a terrorist for a crucial few seconds. Tear gas and smoke may be part of the assault. At every phase the instructors will help the team plan, let them go through a scenario, and then debrief them with withering precision, pointing out even the smallest of failures. Every team member will know their own job to the tiniest detail, as well as their teammates' jobs so they can either take over if necessary or simply stay out of their way and not hinder them.

During their five months of training to join Delta, candidates will go through these exercises time and again until they can perform flawlessly, despite the sound of gunshots and the danger, despite smoke and confusion, and with deadly accuracy, sparing the hostage mannequin while double tapping the terrorist mannequin in the killing house. They will learn to deal with wearing heavy clothing and knee and elbow pads, wearing helmets and gas masks, and they will be ready at any time to intervene in a hostage situation and emerge victorious. They may be split into

Special Forces practicing extractions from a ground mission, via an MH-60G Pave Hawk.

teams, such as a sniping team (consisting of a shooter and a spotter) and an assault team, made up of an entry person, a point man, other shooters, medics, and target designators.

Delta troopers are able to enter combat zones in a wide variety of ways, from SCUBA to HALO, and can also fast-rope out of choppers or rappel down the sides of buildings with equal ease. They will learn to drive motorcycles and cross-country vehicles, such as the modified dune buggies first used in Iraq, or the ATVs that have become popular in the mountains of Afghanistan. It's very hard to keep Delta Force out once they have decided to enter your country, or your city, or your house.

As an essential part of their training they may be attached to other Special Operations Forces units, including, in a nice nod to Colonel Charles Beckwith, the British SAS. They will also learn how to be helpful members of Special Operations Command, working with Special Forces, Navy SEALS, Air Force Special Operations, Rangers, and intelligence agencies such as the CIA who have a paramilitary capability.

And at the end of training they will be members of the ultimate solution to hostage and counterterrorist missions anywhere in the world. They have the men and machines, training and inclination to wade into the most difficult situations and resolve them quickly and violently. They can deploy by a plethora of methods and neutralize terrorists while protecting civilian hostages, while also working with local law enforcement, military and intelligence assets to accomplish their missions with a minimum of fuss and a maximum of resolution.

CHAPTER 7

U.S. Marine Force Recon

*W*hen the United States activated Special Operations Command in 1987, it brought together the finest trained elites of the U.S. Army, Navy, and Air Force into a multifaceted, self-sufficient whole. But then there are "the few, the proud"—the you-know-whos.

The U.S. Marines, already an elite corps of legendary prowess, did not opt to play a role in SOCOM, not because they weren't invited to the party but because they chose not to attend. Thus to all appearances, the new heyday of SpecOps—the greatest since JFK was alive and now with more practical effect—has left the "Old Breed" on the sidelines like xenophobic wallflowers at the global dance. But appearances can be deceiving. Just as the Marines have long had their own air wings and armored battalions, so they also fielded unconventional warriors. Famous throughout the military establishment but little known to the public, the Corps's own Special Operations elites are called Marine Force Reconnaissance.

The primary reason why the Marines have chosen to develop their own resources for independent operations is rooted in history. As a parallel armed forces—the original quick reaction force—capable of rapid deployment around the world, they have traditionally provided U.S. presidents an option to project power without acknowledging a state of war. When the United States mobilizes its army and air force, the entire world spills its coffee. But "sending in the Marines," which has been done literally hundreds of times in our history, is acknowledged as a crisis solver, meant to quell a conflict rather than escalate it. Of course, for half a century now, formal declarations of war have become about as common as slapping your foe's face with a glove in order to fight a duel. And as the world has fragmented since the Cold War, Special Operations Forces in the other services have increasingly been called upon for foreign interventions. Still, the idea of having a separate, self-contained, all-arms corps of elite soldiers is still welcomed by U.S. presidents. And when America—as it frequently does—gets into a hot spot with some serious main-force action on our hands, we always know who to turn to.

Another reason the Marines prefer to stand apart may be rooted in a certain pride. Marines simply don't like to be commanded by the army, and feel there's no reason they should be. Countering the slogan "An Army of one," they have their own credo: "Every Marine is a rifleman." Marine components train as a hard-hitting whole. If their air or armor elements were subordinated to other services or Force Recon subordinated to SOCOM, the thinking goes, these elements would no longer be available to support operations of the Corps. And the Marines have never been ones to jump on a bandwagon. During the 1990s they bucked the trend by refusing to cotton to women within

*In keeping with the Marine credo that "Every Marine is a rifleman,"
Force Recon constantly practices its marksmanship skills. Here a
Marine from Recon gives a combat shotgun demonstration aboard
the USS* Wasp. *(Marine Corps)*

their ranks, while the Clinton administration prudently didn't even bother them with "don't ask, don't tell." When it comes to fighting, however, they've remained at the cutting edge.

The Corps is divided into Marine Expeditionary Forces (MEFs), each of which consists of a division, an air wing, and support elements. Their forward deployments are called Marine Expeditionary Units (MEUs) of some twenty-one hundred men, and these are all now Special Operations Capable (SOC). But while recognizing the Marines as an elite corps in the U.S. military, it would be going a bit far to describe 172,000 men as Special Operations Forces. This is where we come to the Marines's own "elite." Though no one in the Corps uses that word, the rest of the Special Operations world recognizes that it applies to Marine Force Recon.

History

For most of their 227-year history the U.S. Marines weren't concerned with reconnaissance. In the 180 amphibious operations they performed prior to World War II, they sent in advance feelers a few times to satisfy curiosities; but during the musket age the enemy was generally in plain sight. The object was to smash, not scout, and missions were not generally of a strategic nature against major warfighting nations.

World War II thrust the Marines into a new, more vital role. Instead of shipboard auxiliaries for naval actions, they became America's cutting-edge main force against Imperial Japan, with half a million brave young volunteers passing through the Corps during the course of that conflict. Just as the army invented special units from necessity to fight a major war against a powerful, skillful enemy in multivarious terrain, weather, and force-ratio environments, the Marine Corps came up with units of its own to compliment its primary operations. Today's Force Recon has its origins in two concepts from World War II: the Marine Raiders and Amphibious Recon.

The Marine Raiders existed for only two years, but in that short lifespan established a record of courage unsurpassed in American history. The concept was logical enough. By early 1942 the Japanese had swept the British, French, Dutch, and Americans from all their outposts in East Asia. As the United States fell back on its heels among the smoldering ruins of its battleship fleet in Pearl Harbor, Marine Corps Lieutenant General Thomas Holcomb realized that the Americans needed a way to hit back hard and fast. While U.S. forces and industry mobilized what would eventually become overwhelming strength, the enemy could not be allowed to rest. The 1st and 2nd Marine Raider Battalions were formed, respectively, under Lieutenant Colonels "Red Mike" Edson and Evans Carlson. That summer they went into action in the Solomon Islands.

On August 7, the 1st Marine Raider Battalion, supported by a battalion of the 5th Marines, landed on the island of Tulagi. Resistance stiffened as the Raiders moved inland and then the Americans learned how much their enemy coveted the cloak of darkness. That night, Banzai attacks were launched through the jungle, at one point penetrating a company seam. While the Marines piled up Japanese bodies on the perimeter, enemy infiltrators crept through the lines assaulting the medical station, HQ, and other rear elements. Daylight was welcomed with a sigh of relief from the Marines, who proceeded to scour the island. The entire Japanese garrison of 350 men was wiped out, save three who surrendered. The Raiders had lost thirty-eight dead and fifty-five wounded and the 5th Marines had suffered thirty-three casualties. The Raiders then moved to Guadalcanal to play a leading role with the 1st Marine Division in that epic battle.

It had meanwhile been decided to launch the 2nd Marine

Raiders on the kind of independent mission for which the Raiders were designed. On August 17, 1942, the submarines *Nautilus* and *Argonaut* deposited two companies of Raiders off Makin Atoll. The Raiders disembarked from the subs into stormy high seas, finally reaching shore exhausted without much of their equipment. There they fought off Japanese Banzai attacks, endured enemy air raids, and were informed by natives that fresh Japanese troops were arriving by air and sea. That night the Raiders tried to make it back to the subs, which was part of the plan, but the engines on their rubber boats failed against high waves, and most of the men turned back, having lost their weapons. Back on shore, a disconsolate Colonel Carlson decided to surrender. His men found a Japanese soldier and gave him a capitulation note. Meanwhile, other Marines probed the island, killing stray Japanese here and there (including, probably, the one who had received the note) and reported that enemy resistance had evaporated. Unknown to the Raiders they had wiped out most of the garrison during the Banzai attacks. The Americans didn't yet realize that these desperate assaults were not a sign of numerical strength but a last-ditch tactic by the defenders. The next day the subs came in close so the Raiders were able to withdraw, though they accidentally left a dozen men behind. Nine of these were later captured by the Japanese and beheaded.

Though Makin was a mess, it was trumpeted as a great victory back in the States. And the Japanese had now been informed that Marines were liable to land anywhere, at any time. The following month, the 3rd and 4th Marine Raider Battalions were formed and the troops were eventually reorganized into two regiments. In the Central Solomons, Guam, New Georgia, and Bougainville, the Raiders fought on their own or as spearheads of Marine and army assaults. The original two battalions suffered over 100 percent casualties, and the four battalions together suffered 892 dead and over 2,400 wounded.

The end of the Raiders is analogous to the fate of the Army Rangers in Europe. As America gained massive firepower superiority, there was no longer a point in sending daring light combat units behind enemy lines. The Raiders were re-formed as the 4th Marine Regiment. But by coating themselves in heroism from 1942 to 1944 they had provided an invaluable service to the American war effort. Few remember today how at the beginning of the war the Japanese were viewed as supermen: cold, ruthless soldiers that Western arms could not resist. The U.S. Marine Raiders stepped into that gap between perception and reality, taking the battle back to the enemy when the U.S. had no other advantages. They gave better than they got, and informed the world that in terms of raw courage, the Japanese had no edge over the Americans.

Marine Amphibious Recon went into action over a year after the Raiders and were activated for much the same reason as the Raiders disappeared. Once the Japanese tide had crashed into the U.S. breakwater and America had mobilized overwhelming material strength, it was time to head the other way, island-hopping across the vast Pacific in a strategic counteroffensive. The Marines realized they needed a reconnaissance element to explore and decipher the scores of wildly various islands in the Pacific that its main force units needed to control. The navy had already formed Frogmen, or Underwater Demolition Teams (UDTs), to perform recon of reef and beach conditions before launching its landing craft. The Marines's problem was broader in that they needed to identify enemy strength as well as obstacles. They also needed to know which islands needed to be invaded and which could simply be scooped up en route by a few tough Marines who could take care of minor Japanese garrisons by themselves.

The first Marine recon unit of twenty-two men, called the Observer Group, was formed a month after Pearl Harbor under the command of Captain James Logan Jones. It was meant to assist the landings in North Africa but then the plan changed. The army still bridled over the publicity the Marines had earned in World War I and this time were determined that the ETO be an army theater. The Marines could have the Pacific. (At Normandy, the largest, most important amphibious operation in history, only four Marines were present, as observers.)

In January 1943, the Observer Group was expanded into the Amphibious Reconnaissance Company and later that year performed its first mission. Just after midnight on November 21, the company slipped from the submarine *Nautilus* off the shore of Apamama Island, south of Tarawa. In a firefight with the Japanese it suffered its first KIA but the thirty-man enemy garrison was destroyed. More tasks followed and in April 1944 the company was expanded into a battalion, still under the command of Jones. It now employed Assault Personnel Destroyers (APDs) as vehicle of choice.

At Tinian Island in July 1944, an argument broke out between Marine and navy commanders over which beach to assault. Amphibious Recon was slipped onto each beach under cover of darkness where they found that one was heavily fortified with mines, pillboxes, and obstacles, while the other was clear. The invasion subsequently came off without a hitch. (The navy had been mistaken.)

In the western Pacific the Marines employed Coast Watchers, teams that combined Marines, Australians who knew the local terrain and lingo, and sometimes natives. When the Marine Raiders landed for one of their last, and toughest, battles on New Georgia, they were guided ashore by a deep reconnaissance team that had already been in place. During their short career in World

War II, forty-four Amphibious Reconnaissance Marines were killed in action.

With peacetime the recon groups were disbanded, though the concept stayed alive and in 1948 a submarine, the *Perch*, was converted into a transport for training or further recon contingencies. For the Korean War a company was quickly activated and performed a number of raids along with Navy UDTs behind North Korean lines. Another company was created at Camp Lejeune and trained for raids and reconnaissance using APDs, submarines, and rubber boats.

After Korea, the Marines experimented with helicopters, the new invention that allowed inserting force anywhere in the battle zone. Another type of recon unit was created to scout landing zones and perform a Pathfinder role. In June 1957, the air assault recon platoon was merged with 1st Amphibious Recon, Pacific, to form the 1st Force Reconnaissance Company. A cadre was directed east to form the 2nd Force Recon Company, attached to the Atlantic Fleet, which was activated in 1958.

As with the Raiders and Amphibious Reconnaissance units of World War II, the Force Recon companies attracted the best, most daring soldiers in the Corps, which made for an impressive crew, since every Marine was already considered an elite soldier. Force Recon added airborne to its list of capabilities and even pioneered the concept of freefall jumping. It also practiced getting in and out of submerged submarines, SCUBA, small boat maneuvers and rappelling from helicopters, as well as close-quarters combat (with weapons and hand-to-hand), insertion, evasion and other skills needed for behind-the-lines work.

The word "force" in Force Recon is not meant to be synonymous with "power" (though in practice it's not a bad fit) but refers to a Marine Expeditionary Force, differentiating Force Recon from what is usually called Battalion Recon. The latter is

As the Special Operations element of the Marine Corps, Force Recon needs to possess the skills of all the facets of SOCOM. Here a Marine swimmer lets loose from a helicopter over the sea. (Marine Corps)

comparable to the reconnaissance platoons attached to army battalions and are designed for tactical reconnaissance up to ten miles from a unit's position. Force Recon performs strategic missions deep behind enemy lines on behalf of the Force command.

Though by the early 1960s Marine Force Recon had probably become the toughest and most proficient of America's Special Operations Forces it was still relatively unknown except among professionals. (In World War II, commendations for Marine recon troops were marked "Top Secret" because commanders didn't want the Japanese to know they existed.) The Marines were thus jolted in 1962 when the navy, with great fanfare, created its own version of Force Recon, the SEALs. The SEALs, who were formed by adding an air and land capacity to UDT teams, came about partly in response to President Kennedy's new emphasis on unconventional warfare, and partly because the army's Green Berets had become so famous that the navy felt it needed a counterpart. At first, Force Recon didn't even want to train with them, noting that the sailors had an eighteen-month training cycle compared to six for the Marines, who were all tough soldiers to begin with. But shortly the Vietnam War would allow everyone more than enough opportunity to prove their worth.

After the Marines came ashore at Da Nang in March 1965, the Corps took on a major part of the land war, operating in the north. The Marines's eyes and ears were provided by Force Recon, which at the height of the war averaged forty teams in the field. Inserted by helicopter, the four-man teams took up positions overlooking trails or near Communist base camps to track enemy movement. Though their mission was meant to be reconnaissance alone, in practice Force Recon added a combat dimension, springing ambushes and raids on unsuspecting enemy units. A study reported that while 80 percent of Marine infantry engagements were initiated by the enemy, this was true of only 5 percent of Force Recon combats. As a rule, Force Recon attacked and it was the enemy's job to cope with these highly trained warriors who lurked in their midst.

In 1966, it was decided to expand Force Recon's combat role further by backing up the teams with massive fire support. Once a team pinpointed an enemy unit, aircraft were vectored to demolish the target or artillery zeroed in. This program, dubbed "Stingray," meant that a small team could wield the firepower of a regiment. Vietnam being a "body count" sort of conflict, it is worth noting that while Marine infantry achieved a count of 7.6 enemy dead to each of their own, Force Recon's ratio was 34 to 1.

But it all went south, so to speak, as the war dragged on. Force Recon suffered losses and then incurred enmity by trying to recruit the best men from other Marine companies. And as with other Special Operations Forces in Vietnam, the heavily engaged infantry weren't always keen on the mysterious operators who disappeared into the jungle for days at a time. And when SOG started up, recruiting Force Recon Marines for its classified missions, the split between the elite Marines and their "super elites" widened.

When Nixon took office in 1969 he brought a hard-nosed approach to the war, but was compelled to ameliorate it by drawing down U.S. force levels, and especially tried to eliminate casualties. On the ground this threw the entire effort into a slough of confusion as pacification and Vietnamization became more highly prized than battlefield victory. Morale sank and cynicism soared. In March 1969, the 3rd Marine Division was withdrawn from Vietnam and the 3rd Force Recon Company was abruptly disbanded (deactivated the following year). 1st Force Recon continued operations but its numbers dwindled. In August 1970 it was stood down at Da Nang. The company existed on the rolls until September 30, 1974, when it was officially deactivated, its colors furled by its four remaining men. During the war, Force Recon Marines had earned six Medals of Honor.

Fortunately the 2nd Force Recon Company, based in North Carolina, survived Vietnam intact because the Atlantic Fleet still had the Soviets and the Mideast to worry about. Upgrades in training, doctrine, and equipment were thus able to continue, keeping Force Recon abreast of other Special Operations Forces in the 1980s. Coincident with the new geopolitical situation and the creation of SOCOM during Reagan's second term, the Marines reactivated 1st Force Recon.

During Operation Desert Storm in 1991, a combined SOF

force—Army Special Forces, Night Stalker helicopters, and Navy SEALs—stormed the U.S. Embassy in Kuwait City, which had been abandoned by diplomats and then seized by the Iraqi army. After demolishing the place against no opposition they reported that a small American flag had been flying over the embassy when they arrived. This had been placed by Marine Force Recon the day before. The 1st Marine Expeditionary Force had been strictly ordered to halt outside the city and had done so. They simply hadn't seen the need to halt reconnaissance.

In Afghanistan in 2001, the Marines were the first U.S. infantry to arrive in the country, setting up a base called Camp Rhino in the south and securing the Kandahar airport. Force Recon operations have not yet come to light, yet even as these words are written, a ramification from the War on Terrorism has become evident.

In June 2002, the Marines finally elected to send "a few dozen" men to MacGill Airbase, Florida, to serve under Special Operations Command. These men will naturally be members of Marine Force Recon. Though SOCOM now has 46,000 men at its disposal, the addition of these few is a major development. SOCOM will henceforth not only have the Special Operations capability of the army, navy and air force at its disposal but now the U.S. Marines.

To speculate on the reason for this break in the Marines's tradition of self-sufficiency, today's armed forces, due to instant communications, high-speed deployment, and common doctrine, have become increasingly integrated, even as the outside world has fallen into ever smaller fragments. Gone are the days when the Marines alone were America's fast reaction force. And while Marine Expeditionary Units (SOC) continue to stand ready, the probability is that conflicts in the first part of the twenty-first century will favor the deployment of smaller units. In this changed situation the Corps has adjusted. And unfortunately for America's antagonists, they can now expect to see more of the Marines when crises occur, not less of them.

Training

The first thing that strikes you about a Force Recon Marine is a certain modesty. This is not only polite reserve from a fellow who knows good and well he could kill you in a second with his bare hands, but is a philosophy drummed in by the Corps. They are Marines first, and proud to be that. If they are Force Recon, it means they have just assumed a special role to assist fellow Marines, who in any hot war have to do the heavy lifting. Interviewing a Force Recon vet recently, the questioner tried to provoke some emotion. Is there any animosity or envy between the regular Marines and Force Recon? An innocent shrug of the shoulders and shake of the head: "Nah, we're all just Marines." The interviewer persists. Is there competition between you and the SEALs when you visit Coronado? The same innocent shrug and nod: "Nah, we're all just professionals." This humility comes from a six-foot-two guy with about two hundred pounds of pure muscle bulging from his USMC t-shirt. Force Recon doesn't take on airs.

Part of the reason is that the Marines, unlike the other services with their Special Operations Forces, haven't made Force Recon a career specialty. A recruit generally comes from within the ranks of the Marines after three to five years' experience, serves for five years in Force Recon (sometimes with a two-year extension) and then returns to the Corps. There, the skills and knowledge he has gained enhances the whole. In 1998 the Marines began to offer Force Recon as an option to new volunteers, but a period of demonstrated excellence as a Marine is still preferred.

The selection process for Force Recon is heavily weighted to weed out unsuitable applicants at the start. The grueling physical regimen, including running (with packs), push-ups, pull-ups, swimming (with boots), obstacle courses, and then doing everything over again on a moments' notice does a good job of identifying the infirm (or perhaps normal physical specimens). The applicant is also given an exam to test his mental acumen and professional knowledge. He is then assessed by a panel of non-

Ocean-going ship and oil platform takedowns are part of Force Recon's mission, as demonstrated in the Persian Gulf during hostilities with Iran. Here a Marine secures a captured enemy soldier. (Marine Corps)

An instructor watches as a Marine takes aim in a training exercise on the USS Tarawa. (Marine Corps)

coms who have been watching for mental toughness, "gung-ho" spirit, or any intangibles that would mark him as a valuable member of the team.

At least 80 percent of applicants are unable to get through the initial screen. But of those few who pass the Marines's own selection process, interestingly enough, almost 100 percent get through the plethora of additional schools, trials, and courses that follow. The Marines are funded by the navy, which reserves its SOF budget primarily for the SEALs. So more than any other elite unit, Force Recon spreads its training throughout the services, from Ranger School at Fort Benning to Freefall School in Yuma, Arizona, to the Combatant Dive Course at Panama City, Florida. They also take advantage of navy resources at Coronado, California, mountain warfare schools, and Special Forces reconnaissance courses and SERE (Survival, Evasion, Resistance, Escape) School at Fort Bragg. The unspoken rule is that failure is not an option for the Marines representing the Corps at these schools and only injury can keep a Force Recon trainee from passing. At the same time the Marines become keenly familiar with the SOF community. SEAL Team 6, the navy's counterterrorist equivalent to the Army's Delta Force, sometimes solicits Force Recon Marines to join its ranks. Emphasizing, too, the navy's traditional close ties with the Marines, Force Recon's medics are still navy sailors, who undergo the same training, including weapons proficiency, and go through another, separate, ton of schooling besides.

The Marine selection process and the service schools only cover the first two training phases of Force Recon: individual training and working as a unit (platoon). By now a highly skilled team, the third phase is Marine Expeditionary Unit training, lasting six months, which involves performing their skills in coordination with an MEU. Next is deployment, when the Force Recon

Small-boat landings, in addition to SCUBA and airborne insertions, are practiced by Marine recon on both coasts. The imperative is to enter enemy territory silently, quickly, and with lethal force. (Marine Corps)

platoon explores practical contingencies with a forward MEU in the Mediterranean, southern Asia, or Pacific.

Force Recon doctrine has recently evolved from the use of four-man teams, as in Vietnam, to six-man teams. The reasoning is that if a Marine is wounded, the entire team won't be tasked with his extraction; in addition, as high-tech equipment has proliferated, the recon unit should expand to retain its mobility. Any more than six, the Marines believe, would compromise the covert nature of Force Recon missions. Whether they're freefalling, swimming, fast-roping, or marching behind enemy lines, the value of a Force Recon unit is to stay hidden. That way they can perform their primary reconnaissance role, and if combat ensues, it will be Force Recon that initiates it.

CHAPTER 8

U.S. Airborne

*L*eonardo DaVinci's notebooks contain a drawing of a strange-looking square device made of linen that has a man hanging under it. This is one of the first pictures of what was eventually to become the modern parachute, and oddly enough the new ram-air models look more like DaVinci's than the World War II-era circular chutes. But even the visionary Italian inventor and artist might have had a hard time imagining a modern Airborne division, with its potential to drop thousands of heavily armed elite troops from the sky. On the other hand, two restless American thinkers separated by 150 years, Benjamin Franklin and Billy Mitchell, rightly imagined that troops descending from the skies could terrify and overwhelm an enemy.

The Airborne concept is pretty straightforward: just convince young men to willingly jump out of perfectly good airplanes and fall at the rate of over one hundred miles per hour carrying one hundred pounds of weapons and gear until their parachutes open, allowing them to drift to the ground. Once there, the task is to link up with their comrades to undertake tasks of vital importance through rapid tactical moves deep inside enemy territory, where they will remain until they either connect with advancing friendly forces or exfiltrate back to their own lines.

Well that's the theory. In practice, Murphy's Law seems to crop up in the Airborne sphere even more than in ordinary life. The history of parachute operations is riddled with all manner of unforeseen and dangerous turns of events, from confusion on the part of aircraft navigators to poor reconnaissance of the drop zones, to cases of accidentally dropping troops into the ocean. (Though Navy SEALs, USAF Pararescue Jumpers, and select other units are trained to parachute into aquatic environments, it is generally held to be unwise to drop men laden with heavy gear into water.)

There are a few basic parameters to airborne operations. According to the manual, paratroopers are to be dropped fifty to one hundred kilometers behind enemy lines, there to be self-sustaining for seventy-two hours. Confusion will usually reign on all sides, and seventy-two hours can be an eternity once you start shooting people and blowing things up, alerting even the dullest foe to your presence. Airborne troops have no secure rear areas, and once dropped into the middle of an enemy force, if they don't get moving they are quickly the target of a converging opposition.

But central to airborne thinking, in common with all Special Operations Forces, is the ability to improvise, or "adapt and overcome," as they are fond of saying. These soldiers leave behind all the ponderous supply chain that supports an average army on the march, and instead rely on what they can carry. Chief among their assets are quick wits, backed up by their lengthy history and experience of daring operations, and the rigorous training that they must undergo to earn their jump wings.

History

British, Italian, Russian, and German airborne units were exploring the basic tenets of parachute operations by the mid-1930s, and the Soviets released propaganda films of jumps of up to twelve hundred soldiers over Vladivostok. These movies showed men with ordinary flight helmets inching their way out onto the wing of large transport planes such as the ANT-12 and jumping from there to avoid striking the tail section.

There is some debate whether the Nazis used their Fallschirmjaegers in 1939 during the invasion of Poland, but the world was alerted to the potential of these troops the following spring with the invasions of Norway, Holland, and Belgium. The German panzers were preceded by airborne troops—via parachute and glider—who played decisive roles in capturing forts, bridges, and airfields. Blitzkrieg (lightning war) depended on speed, and the job of the German airborne was to neutralize obstacles that could potentially delay the armored columns. A year later the Germans got even more ambitious, launching an invasion of Crete with airborne troops alone.

Some thirty thousand British Empire troops were on the island, backed up by fourteen thousand Greeks and Cretans. On May 21, 1941, seven thousand German paratroopers floated in, joined over the next week by fifteen thousand reinforcements. Just over half the British were able to evacuate by sea while thirteen thousand fell as casualties or surrendered. The world's first strategic campaign waged by airborne appeared to be a success. But the cloud in the silver lining appeared when the German command learned of the utter carnage that had taken place on the drop zones the first day. Entire German companies had been wiped out by waiting machine guns; paratroopers dangling from trees had been knifed by Cretan partisans; men had drifted gently from the sky on top of Aussie bayonets. It was only when a

161

few intrepid paratroopers had managed to seize an airfield that the reinforcement stream commenced. Hitler, appalled at the over six thousand casualties suffered by his elite troops, never launched another major airborne operation.

By 1940 the United States Army had formed its first parachute unit, the 501st Regiment, based at Fort Benning, Georgia, and they set to work making up a doctrine as they trained. In this they were aided by a captured German manual, which pointed them to such things as tumbling and gymnastic training, creating a 250-foot jump tower (such as the one at Coney Island in New York), and the development of "jump boots," whose height and stiffness were needed to protect the paratroopers as they hit the ground. There was resistance from the Quartermasters Brigade over special boots and uniforms, but in time designs for both were tested and issued, including the baggy pants with leg pockets which were bloused over the top of their jump boots in a distinctive style that is still the mark of paratroopers.

By August 1941 the 82nd Airborne Division had been activated, soon followed by the 101st. (The designations were from inactive infantry divisions formed for World War I.) Just eleven months after Pearl Harbor, American 82nd ("All American") Airborne troops in small numbers participated in Operation Torch, the combined forces assault on German-held North Africa. This was the first combat jump in American history, and the beginning of a long tradition of daring Airborne insertions.

But it was the invasion of Sicily (Operation Husky) in July 1943 that revealed both how effective paratroopers could be, and some of the hazards these bold troops needed to confront. Led by legendary paratroop leader Matthew B. Ridgway, the 505th Parachute Infantry Regiment of the 82nd was tasked with landing inland and disrupting communications, as well as preventing enemy reinforcements from reaching the beachheads where the

1st Infantry Division was coming ashore. Tragically, many of the planes transporting them to the island were shot down by their own trigger-happy navy before they even reached the coast. And then many units were dropped in widely dispersed locations (including the Mediterranean Sea). But despite these setbacks, once on the ground the Airborne units sowed confusion and destruction, and served to lessen the effectiveness of the German shore defenses, just as Ben Franklin and Billy Mitchell had predicted. This was also the first use of Pathfinder units, whose job it was to jump in ahead of the main force and mark the DZ ("Drop Zone") with smoke and brightly colored marker panels.

82nd Division paratroopers were also dropped to support the Italian landings at Salerno, and then fought at Anzio, where they became known as the "devils in baggy pants" according to a quote from a German officer. Both sides learned during the war that their paratroopers not only had a unique capability but were among the fiercest of infantry fighters—something about the raw courage and rigorous training that it takes to be a paratrooper.

With the invasion of Europe from England looming as the crucial battle of the war, the airborne operations on D-day were the largest yet. More than thirteen thousand Americans of the 82nd and 101st Airborne Divisions ("The Screaming Eagles") fell from the skies (using gliders as well as parachutes) over Normandy in the dark hours before the amphibious landings of June 6, 1944. (The British 1st Airborne Division also dropped in.) Their assignment was to seize bridges and causeways leading from the beach while seizing or destroying those that led to German reinforcements inland. The planners had predicted a casualty rate of over 70 percent. While thankfully this did not transpire, what did happen was that the paratroopers became scattered from one end of the Cotentin Peninsula to the other. The transports had been shaken by German antiaircraft fire and some pilots dodged, others went too fast, others too slow, and some simply got lost. But an unintended benefit of the wide dispersal was panic and confusion among the Germans, who were seeing paratroopers everywhere they turned.

On the ground, the paratroopers tried to assemble in groups, while company, battalion and even divisional organization was thrown out the window. At one point, General Maxwell Taylor tried to assemble a group of men to seize a causeway and found most of them were officers. "Never have so few been led by so many," he cracked. Taylor's 101st Airborne had lost fifteen hundred men within moments of the drop and 60 percent of the division's equipment. But the fighting qualities and tenacity of the 82nd and 101st made them dangerous even in small numbers, and visionary Airborne leaders and thinkers such as General James M. Galvin of the 82nd had foreseen the potential for this kind of independent action and built it into their training. The amount of mayhem they were able to wreak behind the beaches proved invaluable to the Allied invasion force that soon linked up with their Airborne spearheads. The paratroopers spent the next month fighting as infantry until the enemy front at Normandy finally collapsed.

Just two months later, the American 82nd and 101st Airborne Divisions, the British 1st Airborne, and the Polish Airborne Brigade—some twenty thousand men in all—participated in Operation Market Garden, the daring surprise offensive to propel the Allies into Germany. The plan was for the paratroopers to seize consecutive bridges across rivers—the final one crossing the Rhine at the Dutch city of Arnhem. Armored columns of British XXX Corps would meanwhile blast up the roads, easily traversing the Airborne-held bridges to outflank the enemy's Westwall. On paper it was a brilliant plan.

In practice, unknown to Allied intelligence, the 9th and 10th

After blazing a path of glory across Europe, 82nd Airborne troopers join hands with Russian troops in May 1945, during Nazi Germany's last days. (AP)

SS Panzer Divisions were just then resting and refitting around Arnhem. When the British landed they were immediately surrounded by heavy forces. The Poles, flown in as reinforcements, were unable to effect the outcome. The 82nd Division managed to seize its bridge at Nijmegen, but the 101st was temporarily repulsed at Eindhoven. The Screaming Eagles found a solution by going downriver to flank the Germans in small boats. They lost two hundred men in the crossing but finally took their bridge. The XXX Corps, meanwhile, had been unable to make fast progress, resisted and ambushed by ad hoc German units from the moment it left its startline. In the end, the British 1st Airborne was all but destroyed, the other airborne troops were withdrawn, and Holland remained an inconclusive front for the rest of the war.

It was in the small village of Bastogne during the Battle of the Bulge that the 101st wrote one of the proudest pages in U.S. military history. On December 16, the Germans launched a massive, last-ditch counteroffensive, caving in the American front in the Ardennes. For mobile reserves, the U.S. could only call on its Airborne divisions who were waiting in the rear for their next mission. The 82nd was sent in from the north, where it tried to halt German penetrations around St. Vith. The 101st was trucked over one hundred miles from the south and barely reached Bastogne before it was surrounded by a tidal wave of German armor.

Bastogne was the hub of the road network that the enemy needed to increase its bulge in the Allied front. The 101st, together with elements of the 10th Armored, was surrounded by elements from five German divisions. On December 22 the Germans sent in a request for the Americans's surrender but the 101st's acting commander, Anthony McAuliffe, sent back the one word answer "Nuts!" German artillery hammered the town and panzers sometimes penetrated the perimeter. On Christmas Day, the Screaming Eagles beat off a ferocious attack of tanks and infantry. And then the skies cleared and the Allies were able to reassert their air superiority over the battlefield. Patton's 4th Armored Division broke through from the south, finally relieving the paratroopers. The 101st had once again proven the value of elite forces trained to withstand, and prevail, over more punishment than most units could imagine.

In the Pacific theater, the 11th Airborne Division made two

drops in the Philippines. During the first, at Leyte Gulf, the 187th Regiment was ironically called upon to fend off an enemy airborne drop, the only one the Japanese launched against Americans in the war. After their second drop, on Luzon, the 187th freed an Allied POW camp. The Japanese called the U.S. paratroopers "Rakkasans," which meant "falling umbrellas."

Stationed in the Far East, the 187th, now a Regimental Combat Team, was first on call for the Korean War. In September 1950, when the North Koreans were in headlong retreat before MacArthur's counteroffensive at Inchon, the 187th were dropped thirty miles north of Pyongyang to intercept the fleeing Communist government, escaping enemy troops and, most important, U.S. POWs that might be in transit. The 187th wasn't able to catch the government but they destroyed a regiment's worth of North Korean soldiers. Sadly, they found a train parked in a tunnel with seventy slaughtered U.S. POWs. The following spring the 187th made another large-scale drop, to intercept North Koreans and Chinese fleeing from Seoul, but the Communists had veered in another direction and the 187th caught thin air. Once Korea ceased to be a war of maneuver, airborne operations were discontinued.

But Korea also saw the first widespread use of the helicopter, mostly in a Medevac role. Over the following dozen years the United States explored its combat potential, and by the time the Vietnam War began in earnest, the 101st Airborne Division had switched to choppers. It was now the 101st Air Assault Division. The 11th Airborne Division was disbanded and in 1963 the 187th Regiment joined the Screaming Eagles of the 101st.

Tactically, Vietnam was above all else a helicopter war, and the 101st Air Assault Division arrived in 1965 for what would be a seven-year stay. In 1966 it fought a legendary action at Dak To, coming to the rescue of a surrounded Green Beret/CIDG camp.

Paratroopers of the 101st Air Assault Division escort rescued South Vietnamese prisoners from a jungle POW camp in 1967. Enemy guerrillas had opened up on a patrol of the 101st, leading them to discover the camp, where fifty-one emaciated, disease-wracked South Vietnamese had been kept. (AP)

101st choppers swooped in to evacuate wounded or terrified South Vietnamese. At the same time its own troops took position on the ground; but one unit, C Company of the 502nd Regiment, was placed too far forward. The North Vietnamese 24th Regiment overran the position and C Company called for artillery fire on its own command post. At daybreak, 101st Infantry and choppers pursued the fleeing NVA, but were unable to catch them before they crossed the border.

During the Communists's Tet Offensive in early 1968, the 101st, together with the 1st Cavalry Division, fought the epic battle for Hue, rooting out Communists in the war's only major urban battle. (One platoon had to be dispatched south to the roof of the American Embassy in Saigon, where it helped fight off Viet Cong sappers.) The Tet Offensive also prompted the U.S. command to send in the 82nd Airborne, which in 1965 had been occupied with quelling a dangerous civil war in the Dominican Republic. The jungle canopy of Vietnam was unsuitable for large-scale paratrooper drops, but the 82nd fought for twenty-two months as mobile infantry, deploying from the DMZ in the north to the Mekong Delta in the south until it was withdrawn in December 1969.

The 101st stayed in the country, lending its fire support and air mobile capacity wherever needed. At one point it appeared as if the Screaming Eagles's desire to fight the war conflicted with Washington's desire to draw it down. In May 1969, the 101st decided to root out a built-up nest of NVA regulars in the A Shau Valley. In a bloody ten-day effort they succeeded, driving the enemy from a series of heights. But the battle, dubbed "Hamburger Hill," appalled much of the U.S. public. Afterward, such aggressive operations by U.S. troops were discouraged. In late 1971 and early 1972 the 101st was withdrawn from Vietnam, its combat troops first and its helicopter pilots last.

But it was the helicopter that most affected the Airborne concept in the years to come. In June 1979, the 101st began to receive the new UH-60A Black Hawk. This machine would continually be modified with the stream of new technology pouring from U.S. labs. In April 1980, America suffered its terrible humiliation at Desert One in Iran, and the top pilots of the 101st were asked to volunteer for a new Special Operations outfit, the Night Stalkers (see page 90), which would henceforth give outfits like Special Forces and the Rangers a deep-penetration capacity.

With the introduction of the Black Hawk, to be followed by Pave Hawks and Pave Lows, and the retention of the venerable twin-rotor "Chinook," paratroopers now had new ways to insert men and equipment in the battle zone. These would often pave the way for C-130 "Hercules" aircraft that could bring in light artillery, tracked vehicles, and enough food and supplies to extend the operational limit of airborne offensives. Meanwhile, the 82nd remained an Airborne, as opposed to an Air Assault, division, on call to provide elite fighters from the sky.

In 1983 the 82nd Airborne poured into Grenada on seventeen hours' notice to provide muscle after Army Rangers, in a fairly chaotic parachute drop, had secured the airfield. In 1988 they made a non-combat jump into Honduras that nevertheless illustrated the strategic value of dropping a thousand well-trained and heavily armed men into a threatened country. The Sandanistas of Nicaragua quickly withdrew, choosing not to tangle with the "devils in baggy pants."

Manuel Noriega of Panama wasn't given the option of withdrawing when the 82nd provided six thousand paratroopers in two locations as part of Operation Just Cause. At Torrijos International Airport in Panama City, the 504th Regiment delivered its 1st and 2nd Battalions in the 82nd's first combat jump since World War II. After some hard fighting in the city and countryside, the drug-running Noriega was put behind bars and Panama had been liberated to pursue democracy.

By the time Iraq's dictator Saddam Hussein invaded Kuwait in August 1990, the 82nd Airborne was a well-established "you call, we haul" rapid reaction force. With two thousand gassed-up Iraqi tanks on the border of Saudi Arabia, the emergency was to immediately get U.S. forces into the theater. And the 82nd Airborne Division was first on the scene, if only as a trip-wire or forlorn hope should the Iraqis continue their advance. The paratroopers were soon joined by their 101st Air Assault cousins and eventually by over half a million other troops.

When Desert Shield gave way to Desert Storm, the American-led counteroffensive, the 82nd was attached to the French 6th Light Armored Division on the far left of the allied coalition's

A soldier from the 101st Air Assault Division holds a position during Operation Apache Snow II in Afghanistan in June 2002. The operation, intended to root out Al Qaeda and Taliban forces, took place ten miles from the Pakistani border. (AP)

famous left hook. The paratroopers advanced in vehicles, at the edge of the turning movement that quickly collapsed the enemy front. Meanwhile, the 101st Air Assault was making the largest helicopter assault in history, employing three hundred choppers to penetrate one hundred and ten miles into Iraq to cut off the escape of Saddam Hussein's Republican Guard. Using Apache attack helicopters as well as troop carriers, the Screaming Eagles captured thousands of enemy troops and then jumped fifty miles more to block another avenue of escape with firepower.

At every step of their illustrious history, whether by dropping from the skies to surprise the enemy, or fighting vicious confrontational battles in hedgerows, jungles, deserts, or cities, U.S. Airborne forces have remained the premier main-force option America can deploy—in under twenty-four hours— to contest any aggressor. It's easy to see why one of the mottos of the paratroopers is "All The Way!"

Training

The toughness of Airborne training has always been uncompromising. The army is not in the business of handing out those little wings to just anybody. The 82nd Airborne is set to deploy to anywhere in the world with eighteen hours notice, and to get to that level of readiness, they work hard and train harder. The average paratrooper can count on 270 training days a year, will run about seven hundred miles in those twelve months and make twelve parachute jumps.

Because of the very nature of their specialty, and the fact that Airborne troops may be asked to fight and travel at a moment's notice in some of the worst places in the world, it only makes sense to demand the highest levels of fitness, with minds attuned to carry out orders without hesitation as well as have the ability to think on one's own and make hard decisions in the absence of higher authority. It's a tall order, and it all starts with Jump School.

Airborne training is a three-week process open to men and women who are at the highest standard of physical fitness and have a good record in their military careers. The base at Fort Benning, Georgia, has been the home of Airborne training since 1940.

AAT (Army Airborne Training) begins with filling out DA Form 4187 (Personnel Action) with required enclosures. Recruits are required to meet or exceed the following APFT (Army Physical Fitness Test) standards: forty-two push-ups in less than two minutes, fifty-three sit-ups in less than two minutes, and running two miles in under fifteen minutes and fifty-four sec-

Today, all Special Operations Forces are expected to be Airborne-qualified. Airborne training, however, requires rigorous physical training as well as jumps.

onds. Once the paperwork is in order and they have demonstrated their ability to perform at the necessary physical levels, recruits wait for the call to report to Fort Benning, where three weeks of progressively more challenging training culminates in five static-line jumps. A static line is a system where soldiers are attached to the plane by a breakaway line that deploys their parachute after they have fallen a bit away from the aircraft. Pulling your own ripcord is an advanced technique reserved for those who will progress to HALO (High Altitude, Low Opening) free fall jumps.

But before they start pushing recruits out of planes, Ground Week comes first, where physical fitness is honed by formation running at an average pace of seven to nine miles per hour. Tower Week is next, where they practice jumping off successively higher platforms, culminating in the three-story jump tower, which slides them down a wire to simulate an actual jump. Finally comes Jump Week, where all their training culminates by having them actually hook up and stand in the door, anxiously watching their Jump Master, until he gets the green light from the pilot indicating they are somewhere close to their DZ (Drop Zone). Then, with an unequivocal "GO! GO! GO!" they step into the breeze generated by the propeller-driven airplane traveling at 120 knots and fall from about fifteen hundred feet like a stone, at least to begin with.

All things being equal, their plummet is arrested by their main canopy opening up and slowing them down. But they have been trained to look up and check their chute, and if it's what they call a "ball of garbage" (a parachute that has deployed but is not forming the happy circle or square that means it's working correctly), then they rapidly go to their reserve chute, which cuts away the main and deploys a spare. Hopefully, all this happens above five hundred feet, which is close to the limit for a parachute to open up and prevent you from being driven into the ground like a spike. "Glory, glory, what a hell of a way to die," as Airborne troops sing to the tune of "The Battle Hymn of the Republic."

Even in still air, parachutes will still plop them on their butts at about twenty feet per second and any wind will increase this speed. But hopefully they have absorbed their training and learned to roll as they land to prevent breakage. If the wind is up, they won't have time to revel in their survival, because those gentle breezes can catch their deployed chute on the ground and drag them away if they don't collapse the canopy and get unhooked from it. Fast release buckles help with this. Then of course they are free to see if there are any men who look like them anywhere around, and try to figure out where they are, where the objective is, and how they are going to get there. And all of that is just to get them to where the enemy can take a shot at them.

Equipment

The equipment carried by paratroopers has always been dictated by the method of their arrival in the combat zone. Starting in World War II, U.S. Airborne forces began testing a new generation of uniforms and weapons from the ground up, and the qualities they were looking for mirrored the paratroopers who were to use them: durability, light-weight, hard-hitting, and fast. Since zippered pockets on jump blouses got jammed with dirt, they were replaced with snaps. When the handy M-1 .30-caliber carbine needed to get to the ground in a smaller package, a folding wire stock was fitted. Even today the Airborne troops remain in the forefront of weapons testing and development, always looking for the next piece of gear that will make their job that much easier, and promote their deadly rapidity on the battlefield.

Men of the 82nd Airborne Division shown with "Own the Night" goggles attached to their helmets. American troops have historically avoided nocturnal battles, but have recently, through technology, become the best nightfighters in the world. (AP/Bob Jordan)

The T-10 parachute, the current issue, is a circular ("parabolic") piece of fabric that has been used since the 1950s and is supposed to be rated for 250 pounds. There are also two steerable parachutes, the MC1-1B and the MC-1C, which have some materiel taken from the rear to make them respond to toggles on the risers, allowing for a degree of maneuverability in the air.

Thirty suspension lines, each twenty-five and a half feet long, connect the paratrooper to his means of safe descent, and the parachutes are repacked every 120 days to make sure they are ready to go when you leave the airplane.

But the load of the paratrooper has been steadily growing, and when you think of the rucksack between their legs (to be let down on a special line before landing), the reserve parachute on the chest, and the T-10 on their back, along with an M16 rifle, perhaps with a 40mm grenade launcher under the main barrel, or the SAW (Squad Automatic Weapon, the Belgian MiniMi), anti-tank rockets, a bayonet, food and supplies for seventy-two hours, and a host of small items from GPS to canteens, you can see why there have been ongoing efforts at developing smaller and lighter gear. There has been a push for a new parachute, and the XT-11 is slated for introduction in 2004. There is also continual controversy on everything from the need for a better chin strap for the helmet, to the use of special militarized mountain bikes, and an ongoing debate over wheels versus tracks. Vehicles are an essential piece of the mobility puzzle, but they have to be able to be landed by either parachute or on pallets that are pushed out the rear door of a C-130.

There are also special 105mm and 155mm lightweight airborne artillery howitzers, which can use modern ammunition to make up in punch what they lack in size, and the entire range of modern communication and navigational gear, including satellite phones and Global Positioning Satellite units for pinpoint accuracy.

The 82nd Airborne Division is based at Fort Bragg, North Carolina. The fourteen thousand men and women of the 82nd are on a "cycle system" whereby they rotate through training and support roles, with the last third on orders to be able to deploy anywhere in the world in less than a day. Their instant response times in the Grenada and Desert Shield Operations, and their high level of training ensures that they are one of the primary "go to" options of any United States president in need of an armed presence abroad.

The 101st Air Assault Division is based at Fort Campbell, Kentucky, and comprises three brigades of troops, along with an entire galaxy of attack helicopters and troop movers, and all the people needed to keep them going, from mechanics to cooks. The roughly twelve thousand men of the 101st train every day to work with their technologically demanding mode of assault, and their use in every sector of the globe attests to their spirit and flexibility.

CHAPTER 9

10th
Mountain
Division

*F*rom Kings Mountain in the Revolution to Lookout Mountain in the Civil War to Tora Bora in the Hindu Kush, American armies have always fought for the heights. Mountain warfare presents unique challenges, such as limited means of communication, extreme weather, the use of small groups instead of massed forces, and the need to carry gear and weapons up and over imposing rocky crests, using everything from skis to snowshoes and crampons (spikes for traction worn over boots). Mountaineering is difficult enough, but when you add a combat dimension you get a branch of warfare that is unforgiving by any standard. The specialized unit of the United States Army that is trained for mountain and arctic warfare is the 10th Mountain Division, based at Fort Drum, New York. By the very nature of its training and operations, as well as its legacy of combat, the 10th Mountain is a unique force. While proving its mettle from the Apennine Range in Italy to the forbidding mountains of

On one of the first days of Operation Anaconda in Afghanistan members of the 10th Mountain Division prepare for battle in the heights of Afghanistan. (AP/U.S. Army/David Marck)

Afghanistan, the skills and the esprit de corps of the mountain troops have overcome obstacles that would flummox a less specialized force.

History

Mountaineering in the United States began in New England with the establishment of a trail network that still offers rugged hiking to enthusiasts. But the pursuit of mountain sports in winter didn't begin to gather steam until the 1930s. The Winter Olympics at Lake Placid in 1938 were an eye-opener for most Americans, while at the same time ski instructors from Europe began to arrive in the U.S. as refugees from the Nazis. Organizations like the AMC and Sierra Club suddenly grew from humble beginnings to prominence, encouraging responsible use of mountains with emphasis on hard training, carrying the right gear, and being prepared to evacuate yourself if necessary—values that mountaineers still live by. Because of the remoteness and isolation of mountains, a certain dauntless ethos came to characterize those who climbed and skied in all weather. The gear was primitive, including arcane-looking hickory skis and leather boots, and the clothing was all wool, but the mountaineers displayed an attitude that could be described as "cautious audacity." After all, just as with the ocean, you never really beat a mountain or conquer a winter storm—the best you can do is work within the fierce parameters of nature to accomplish your objectives.

Even before the United States entered World War II, the importance of mountain warfare had been glimpsed by a few visionary thinkers such as Charles Minot ("Minnie") Dole, founder of the National Ski Patrol. Dole began to lobby for the creation of a specialized American mountain unit, offering the entire resources of the NSP to the U.S. Army. "It is more reason-

181

able to make soldiers out of skiers," he said, "than skiers out of soldiers." Fortunately, army chief of staff George C. Marshall had done a bit of mountaineering himself, and was familiar with the difficult conditions and unique mindset that came with the territory. As both men observed the new European war that had begun on September 1, 1939, the need for American mountain troops became clear.

In Europe, the concept of mountain troops and warfare had begun much earlier. The French had their legendary Chasseur Alpins, formed in the 1830s and based in the Mont Blanc region, while the British had set up a mountain warfare school in the Scottish Highlands, staffed by Commando instructors. The Germans, Austrians, and Italians had all created well-trained and highly regarded mountain troops who had fought vicious battles in northern Italy during World War I; and the Germans had such achievements as the first ascent of the dreaded North Face of the Eiger in Switzerland to their credit, accomplished after many deadly failed attempts by off-duty troops. The North Face remains one of the most forbidding tests of mountaineering skill, rewarding speed and intelligence, and punishing the unprepared with death by avalanche or falling.

The war between Finland and Russia in 1939 was closely watched by mountaineers in the U.S., particularly when reports arrived of small Finnish ski units ghosting through the mountains and forests to wreak havoc on Soviet infantry and armor. Dressed all in white, and having spent their entire lives with the harsh realities of cold and snow, the Finns were able to hold off the enemy for most of the winter. The Soviets finally prevailed but lost as many as a million men, mainly to cold and starvation after Finns had slipped behind invading columns to sever their supply lines.

The Germans went into World War II with a number of

mountain (Gebirgs) divisions and in 1942 formed the 20th Mountain Army to fight in the far north. Commonly known as the Lapland Army, it included Finns as well as army and SS mountain and ski troops. The most crucial use of mountain troops in the war, however, came in the summer of 1942 when the Germans reached the Caucasus Mountains, a range higher than the Alps that stood astride the Soviet Union's oil-producing region. The German 1st and 4th Mountain Divisions invaded the heights, engaging in vicious high-altitude combat with tenacious Soviet defenders.

But then came one of the hazards of forming military units from sporting enthusiasts. The German mountaineers eventually fought their way to 18,500-foot Mount Elbrus. This was the highest peak in the Caucasus and one of those Holy Grails that Alpinists can't resist. A combined party of the Germans's best climbers scaled the mountain, whereupon they proudly planted their divisional flags and the German national flag on top. The Nazi propaganda ministry broadcast pictures of the exploit worldwide, but Adolf Hitler was reportedly intensely annoyed. The Battle of Stalingrad had just begun, he was staring calamity in the face, and there were his elite mountain troops caught on camera goofing off. Of course the Soviets were no better. When their counteroffensive came through the area one of their top priorities was to scale Mount Elbrus themselves, to take down the German flags and run up their own.

Thanks to foresight, on December 8, 1941, the first day after Pearl Harbor, the 87th Mountain Infantry Battalion was activated at Fort Lewis in Washington state. From this seed was to grow the 10th Mountain Division. The 87th used two ski lodges on Mount Ranier, and at one point the battalion thought (mistakenly) that they had accomplished the first winter ascent of that formidable, 14,400-foot mountain. Meantime they had begun the process of learning how to carry all the gear and weapons of a modern army into zones where few armed forces were capable of operating.

As the Americans began to expand their mountain capabilities, the search for a central training base settled on Camp Hale in the Pando Valley of Colorado. At 9,200 feet above sea level, the first difficulty at that altitude was simply adjusting to the lack of oxygen. Modern travelers know that simply visiting Denver, the "Mile High City," can mean a couple of days of headaches and lethargy. For those who don't spend time getting used to the lack of oxygen, HACE and HAPE (High Altitude Cerebral Edema and Pulmonary Edema) await as potentially life-threatening conditions. Altitude has many annoying features, rendering food tasteless, disturbing sleep, and making frostbite and frostnip all the more likely. Add in howling wind, dampness, and dizziness, and it's a wonder that anyone ever leaves sea level. But most of the enlisted men at Camp Hale, if not the officers, were already experienced, and the lumbermen, skiers, and climbers shared all their tips and tricks. The unit's task, in fact, was not only to survive but to overcome all physical obstacles to form a hard-charging and hard-hitting unit that could ascend frozen peaks with weapons and ninety-pound packs in any weather to engage the enemy.

The 10th Light Division (Alpine), consisting of the 85th, 86th, and 87th Regiments, was activated at Camp Hale on July 15, 1943. "Minnie" Dole had tapped the entire American Alpinist community, and the division's ranks included world champion ski jumper Torger Tokle (who was later KIA), Olympic medalist Robert Livermore, and Werner von Trapp (one of the kids made famous in the *Sound of Music*). Also in the ranks were the men who would eventually found the Aspen and Vail, Colorado, ski resorts, as well as Bill Bowerman who founded the Nike sneaker company. Since skiing was then an upper crust kind of sport, the division had the highest proportion of collegiates and high IQs in the army. But there weren't quite enough of those to fill out the 15,000-man establishment, so men were also dragooned from other units. Another fellow named Dole, twenty-two-year-old Robert from Kansas, was one of those who was told by his recruiting officer he'd just "volunteered" for the ski troops.

Despite its hard training and elite skills, however, none of the U.S. theater commanders really wanted the division. It was large but had no heavy weapons companies. Instead of a full complement of vehicles it had hundreds of mules for transport. The United States was then involved in amphibious operations in both the Atlantic and Pacific. Where would the ski troops (and their mules) fit in? As the division remained stateside, morale took a beating. The lengthy waiting period was difficult, but it also banded the men together with hoops of iron as they shared the primitive living conditions of Camp Hale and participated in increasingly difficult mountain maneuvers.

Every phase of high-altitude warfare was explored, and the modern version of the snowmobile, snow cat, and telemark ski were all to owe their development to the men of the 10th. Men who had worked outdoors in the north such as timber cruisers and telephone linemen had made a few strange contraptions for using gasoline engines to move across level snowfields, and most of these were of the "Model T with treads" design. But at Camp Hale the Weasel saw its debut as a tracked people mover capable of thirty to forty miles per hour travel where the terrain would permit its use. The telemark ski also came into its own, being a compromise between the standard downhill ski, with the boots locked onto the ski, and the cross-country ski with its heel free to aide in striding. To ascend on skis, men strapped fish-scale coverings on, which dug in when stationary, but could slide forward when going uphill. Telemark skiing with a heavy pack is a dodgy proposition, but with a fair amount of practice (and some spectacular falls) it is possible to gracefully and quickly descend even steep slopes. But it is a skill that few are born with. To aid in their mission, many of the things we take for granted today in the outdoors were invented or improved during this phase of the division's history, including pile garments, down sleeping bags and clothing, nylon climbing rope, dehydrated food, small and efficient cooking stoves, and new standards for testing gear to the level needed on a frozen peak in combat. Robert Bates and Captain Albert Jackman came up with a new boot that could be used for skiing, rock climbing, or hiking, activities which had previously required three different boots.

The culmination of all this training and innovation were the "D-Series" division-level maneuvers, during which twelve thousand men lived and fought skirmishes in the field, but in this case the field was the unrelenting Rocky Mountains of Colorado. For six weeks the 10th operated at around thirteen thousand feet in blizzards and howling wind, as the temperature dropped to as low as thirty below. On the worst day, one hundred men fell to frostbite. There were those who suggested only half in jest that combat was almost as tough as the "D-Series." But from this crucible of snow and ice came a division undaunted by vertical terrain who could work with the mountains and the weather to not only overcome staggering obstacles, but also be a highly effective fighting force once the summit was reached. Their motto was: "We Climb to Conquer."

That summer the division moved to Texas for further training, adding two thousand men, more mules, and heavy weapons companies. At this stage it was redesignated the 10th Mountain Division. But frustration grew over lack of deployment overseas. When a request came in to replace Airborne losses at Normandy, so many men volunteered that the division cancelled all transfers. Even when the amphibious operations in Europe had ended by fall 1944, the men still trained. It's possible, in fact, that all the toffs and celebrities in the division discouraged U.S. Army commanders from wanting it on their hands.

But the call finally came in from General Mark Clark's 5th Army in Italy. Clark had expected to sweep through the Italian boot after Salerno, then Anzio, or at least once he had conquered Rome. Instead, the Germans were still holding him up along a succession of mountain ranges running east-west across the peninsula. No strangers to mountain warfare, the Germans were constantly forcing the attackers to fight uphill, wading through mine fields, pre-plotted artillery, and withering crossfire to even come to grips. In addition, Clark had been stripped of manpower priority after the invasions of France, and his theater was now a hodgepodge of international units drawn from India to Brazil. In the 10th Mountain Division, morale suddenly soared because they were finally going overseas.

The division arrived in Italy at the end of January 1945. Blocking the way to the strategic Po Valley were a series of German-held mountains connected by ridges. Previous 5th Army attempts on these fortified heights had failed and the task was handed to the 10th. By February they had a plan that came directly from their mountain heritage. Scouts on skis had gone ahead and located five separate routes up a feature called Riva Ridge, and on the night of February 18 the seven hundred men of the 1st Battalion, 86th Infantry Regiment (with one company from the 87th) conducted a daring attack in the dark, climbing eighteen hundred feet from the river valley below. The German battalion guarding the summit had assumed that no attackers could approach from that direction, and as a result the summit was taken quickly without a preliminary artillery barrage or any of the usual preludes to an attack. When you study the map and look at the photographs, and then imagine trying to get seven hundred men up that cliff in winter darkness without making a sound, you can begin to understand why the 10th Mountain Division is a special force. The Germans counterattacked repeatedly, but the men of the 10th dug in and held on. In the following days they constructed an aerial tramway that took their wounded soldiers down the mountain, and brought five tons of supplies up. They then attacked another height, Mount Belvedere, again in darkness and without artillery support. The men were ordered to climb without loading their weapons (so as not to give away their positions with fire) and to rely on only grenades, bayonets, and knives. They surprised another German battalion, took the height, and then held off seven German counterattacks. Repulsing the enemy, the mountain troops then attacked along the ridge to the northeast. The enemy fell back, assuming rightly that they had been hit by elite Alpine troops.

In the following weeks, the 10th Mountain Division continued to fight vicious combats as they pushed the Germans out of the Appenines. On April 14, young Lieutenant Bob Dole was badly wounded. After a couple years in a hospital he would go on to be vice president of the United States and then a candidate for the presidency in 1996. During that same operation, a 10th trooper won the Medal of Honor. Private John Magrath was pinned down with his unit by machine-gun nests, but somehow managed to charge and take one of them, turning the captured weapon on other enemy troops, and he led a sweep that wiped out four nests in all. Later that day he volunteered to run and get a casualty report, and was killed by two mortar shells that landed at his feet.

When the Allies finally broke into the clear in Italy, the 10th was the first unit to reach the Po River. This had been unexpected by 5th Army so they had to wait for boats. Then they were the first unit to cross. By that time the Germans were surrendering in droves. William O. Darby of Ranger fame had been named assistant division commander of the 10th in the last days so he would officially be in line for further promotion. In a weird event, during the last full day of the war in Italy, Darby was finishing a conference in a peaceful, liberated village when a German 88mm shot came out of nowhere and killed him. Overall, in its 114 days in combat, the 10th suffered 5,146 combat casualties, 992 of them KIA.

With the end of the war the 10th Mountain Division was deactivated, but then returned as an infantry training unit in 1948 based at Fort Riley, Kansas. In 1954, with a logic exclusive to the denizens of the Pentagon, the personnel of the 37th Infantry Division became the 10th Mountain Division, but then the division was deactivated again in 1958.

It was not until 1985 that some clever person foresaw the need for mountain troops, and the 10th Mountain Division (Light Infantry) was once again in business, based at Fort Drum, New York. But its capability was not limited to heights. For Operation Desert Storm, twelve hundred men of the 10th Mountain deployed in support of the U.S. 24th Mechanized Regiment. The year 1992 brought a different type of mission, indicative of the range of versatile tasks that would be asked of this light infantry division. A monstrous hurricane swept in from the Atlantic and pounded Florida, causing thirteen deaths and leaving an estimated 250,000 people homeless. Part of the response to the catastrophe was Task Force Mountain, in which six thousand men from Fort Drum set up shop in what was essentially a war zone, and worked quickly to provide food, shelter, and medical aid to the devastated victims. Proving once again that special training breeds adaptable troops, the men of the 10th spent a month in Florida helping to stabilize the population, and then to help rebuild some of the $20 billion worth of damage.

Now considered one of the army's premier Quick Reaction Forces, the 10th Mountain next found itself in Somalia as the headquarters unit of Operation Restore Hope, the effort to feed an entire population wracked by famine. In May 1993 the U.N. took over the operation but 10th Mountain troops stayed in the area, 7,300 of its personnel eventually serving in the effort. At one point, engineers from the 10th constructed a 160-foot Bailey Bridge to open a corridor for supply, the longest such structure constructed by U.S. troops since Vietnam. Much of their time was spent providing security on roads and in cities around Somalia, where the population was ruled by lawless warlords who held power through the use of armed thugs and roaming "technicals," pickup trucks with a machine gun mounted in the bed. This was a new type of war in which light infantry would be faced with exceptional difficulties, confronted with operations involving both humanitarian aid and providing order against predators. In anarchic Somalia, warlords had begun to prey on the population, seizing food and medical supplies to enhance their own position.

In October 1993, Task Force Ranger swooped into the capital, Mogadishu, to seize lieutenants of an especially vicious warlord, Farah Aidid. But two U.S. Black Hawk helicopters went down (two more crippled) while the Army Rangers and Delta operatives became surrounded by thousands of hostile Somalis in the center of the city. Malaysian and Pakistani peacekeepers responded to the crisis, but the 10th Mountain was America's own Quick Reaction Force. Its men fought through gauntlets of enemy fire to help pull the Special Operations Forces to safety. The division suffered one dead and twenty-nine wounded during the battle.

The following year, the 10th Mountain Division executed the largest army operation ever launched from an aircraft carrier. Two thousand men carried by fifty-four helicopters landed in Port Au Prince, Haiti, to help restore calm to a volatile populace

10th Mountain troops participating in Operation Iron Fist in Kosovo in December 2001. The soldiers have just finished a weapons search in nearby villages and are waiting extraction by helicopter. (AP)

on the brink of civil war. Of 21,000 troops eventually contributed by twenty nations to quell that incipient conflict, 8,600 were from the 10th Mountain Division. In 1997, the 10th was tasked with operations in war-torn Bosnia, deploying its engineers and three thousand other troops to a land of cold and snow that had been wracked with ethnic conflict. During the 1990s, the operational tempo of the 10th Mountain Division was unsurpassed by any other division in the army.

And in September 2001, when the United States suffered the greatest surprise attack in its history, the 10th Mountain was among the first to get the call. Units of the division immediately deployed to bases in Uzbekistan, north of Afghanistan, as part of Operation Enduring Freedom. In March 2002, 10th Mountain

10th Mountain troops occupy an Afghan compound, made from the same kind of mud brick seen by Alexander the Great. The soldier on the ladder has fixed an M203 40mm grenade launcher to his M-16. (AP/Pool, Joe Raedle)

was the primary unit involved in the operation's largest battle fought by U.S. troops, in the Shah-i-Kot Valley. To the many veterans of the 10th Mountain Division, it must have seemed like old times again, albeit with the latest in GPS navigation, air support, hi-tech reconnaissance, and an enemy who, while renowned as mountain fighters, were unable to match the training and grit of the 10th.

Training

The men (and now women) of the 10th retain their "Mountain" designation, but they no longer wait for campaigns among the heights. They are instead more like the model of a new army, one that can operate in diverse conditions, from the Mideast to the Caribbean, performing Civil Action in the States as easily as probing the hills of the former Yugoslavia. And of course they are always ready for a shot at the Hindu Kush.

Training takes place at Fort Drum in upstate New York, at the Ethan Allen Firing Range in the mountains of Vermont, and at Fort Greely in Alaska, where the unrelenting conditions are perfect for training mountain troops. But today, most non-mechanized units of the army receive mountain training, as do Special Operations Forces, and one of the tasks of the 10th is to provide Opposing Force (OpFor) troops in exercises and wargames at installations from Alaska to Quebec, as well as at the Army Mountain Warfare School in Vermont. Today's mountain training includes the use of snow skis, snowshoes, ahikio sleds, rappelling (up and down a sixty-foot ice wall) and vehicles similar to snowcats called Small Unit Support Vehicles. This is in addition to the runs, hikes, and marches in the most trying terrain the instructors can find.

As the army's premier Quick Reaction Force among infantry, the 10th is also schooled in the latest gadgets, or Advanced Warfighting Equipment, coming off the drawing boards of America's scientists. These include "Own The Night" goggles, continually enhanced and now providing 3-D; advanced Mortar Fire Control Systems; the Global Positioning Systems for navigation; and such experiments as the Dismounted Soldier System, based on an IBM Thinkpad. The 10th have also worked with an exotic device that continually tracks heartbeat, body temperature, and other physical signs so

A soldier is trained in rappelling at the 10th Mountain's base at Fort Drum in upstate New York. (AP)

that a medic will know when a trooper's been hit or is on the verge of hypothermia.

With their gallant, can-do service in Afghanistan under their belt, the training cycle of the 10th will go on. Mountains all across the land will witness units of the 10th training for wherever they may next be called to serve. Because about 40 percent of the world is mountainous, we can be sure that the skills they possess will be useful. The old lessons haven't been forgotten. You still need to have good boots, keep them dry, have a change of socks, use a layering system to keep warm and out of the wind, use map and compass to find your way, and practice safety at all times while traversing the heights. Added to that, the soldiers of the 10th will carry their heavy packs and weapons, be proficient in the use of snowshoes, skis, and climbing gear, and also have the ability to operate as small groups to move quickly over the rocky terrain that is their home. If helicopters or vehicles can get in, they will use them—otherwise they will climb, just as did the original members of their unit, and on those treacherous slopes they will conquer.

CHAPTER 10

U.S. Coast
Guard
Special
Operations

*T*here's an ocean-going service that is older than the U.S. Navy, answers fifty thousand calls for help each year in all weather and sea conditions, and deploys "rescue swimmers" and aviation assets that are reminiscent of Navy SEALs and Air Force Pararescue Jumpers. That service is the Coast Guard, and in the new world of homeland security and threats to the American coast, they are heading, to an unprecedented degree, toward being enfolded into the military forces of the United States. Coast Guard intelligence has been given a place in the national security pantheon, and the navy has just transferred a dozen 170-foot Special Operations ships to Coast Guard control—both signals that this often overlooked branch of the service is about to assume a greater role in both security and Special Operations work.

History

The "Revenue Cutter Service" was created in 1790 by Alexander Hamilton, and because the Continental Navy was disbanded at the end of the Revolution and not started up again until 1794, this makes the Coast Guard the oldest continuous seagoing force in America. Many of her officers were Continental Navy veterans, and there has always been a connection between the two services, but most often with the Coast Guard on the lower end of budget and manpower. The Coast Guard has nevertheless led the way in pioneering small craft operations, including the Life Saving Service of the 1800s that performed staggering feats of heroism in the rescue of shipwrecked mariners close to shore. Using line-guns and breeches buoys, as well as oar-powered lifeboats, they went out in some of the worst storms ever witnessed on these shores and more often than not returned with men who were soaked to the skin, frozen to the bone, and facing imminent death. The bravery and laconic attitude of these life savers toward their responsibilities was expressed by a saying that persisted almost up to the present day: "You have to go out; you don't have to come back."

The Coast Guard also has many fascinating tidbits hidden away in its history, such as the first U.S. ship to be commanded by an African-American officer (1st Lieutenant Michael Healy in 1877), the first hostile shot fired in the Civil War (Charleston Harbor, 1861), the first drug interdiction boarding (of an opium vessel in 1890), and the first use of aviation in national law enforcement (an airplane that spotted and helped in the capture of a rum-runner in 1925). Coast Guardsmen based at Kill Devil Hill in North Carolina also provided companionship and support to the Wright Brothers during the windy winters on the Outer Banks when they were perfecting the first powered airplane (1903). While working quietly and on guard twenty-four hours a day, seven days a week, throughout the year, the Coast Guard is easily overlooked, but when you start to appreciate the job they do day in and day out, and then compare and contrast them with better known Special Operations Forces, it becomes clear that because of their nautical expertise and role as ocean-going SWAT teams, as well as having more search-and-rescue (SAR) experience than any other branch, they are a special unit that is bound to have a more prominent role in the future.

Their record in combat is illustrious but, typically, little remembered. In the War of 1812 the cutter *Surveyor* fought such a brisk (if losing) action against the British frigate Narcissus that the British captain returned the sword that had been surrendered to him, along with a letter expressing his amazement at the bravery of the American sailors. Also during that conflict, the cutter *Eagle* showed indomitable will when, even though it was forced aground on the coast of Long Island, its crew took their cannon ashore and continued the fight, even using their log book as wadding and recovering British roundshot to fire it back.

The Revenue Cutter Service and the Life-Saving Service were merged as the U.S. Coast Guard in 1915, and in 1917 the new service was attached to the navy for American participation in World War I. The majority of craft were based in Gibraltar during the war, tasked with escorting British ships between there and the United Kingdom. One cutter, the USS *Tampa*, accomplished eighteen missions, escorting some 350 Allied ships safely before being sunk by a German U-boat off the English coast.

In 1940 the United States was once again preparing for conflict, this time on a global scale. The Coast Guard's duties would include port security in America as well as patrolling the sea lanes both near the U.S. and along the dangerous convoy routes to Britain. With their experience on the International Ice Patrol (set up after the *Titanic* catastrophe in 1912), the Coast Guard was

Coast Guard coxswains steer Marines toward the beaches of Saipan in June 1944. Coast Guardsmen participated in every major Pacific invasion during World War II. During the D-day invasion of France, they plucked 1,500 struggling soldiers from the waters off Normandy. (Coast Guard)

well prepared to operate off the frozen coasts of Greenland and Iceland, as well as trying to halt the epidemic of U-boat attacks along the American East Coast, some of them within sight of land. In November 1941, one month before Pearl Harbor, the Coast Guard was once again attached to the navy, and went on to lend its seagoing expertise and SAR abilities to every major operation of World War II in both the Atlantic and the Pacific. Cutters were able to sink eleven German submarines, and one more was destroyed from the air. Coast Guardsmen provided both direct CSAR (Combat Search & Rescue) and training for hundreds of small craft operators who would participate in the war's amphibious landings. On D-day, the Coast Guard managed to save fifteen hundred men cast into the cold waters off the coast of Normandy. On that day alone they deployed sixty 83-foot patrol craft. The U.S. Coast Guard won one Medal of Honor and six Navy Crosses during World War II while lending 802 cutters to the war effort, as well as providing port security and coastal patrol on American shores.

During the Korean War, as well as acting as a safety net for the thousands of United Nations troops being flown and floated

The Coast Guard in South Vietnam, 1965. An 81mm mortar round has just exploded above a suspected Viet Cong cave near Da Nang. The .50-caliber machine gun mounted above the mortar has also been fired into the cave. (Coast Guard)

to the Korean peninsula, fifty members of the Coast Guard helped to set up the South Korean Coast Guard, which became the South Korean Navy. This educational role is reminiscent of the task of Army Special Forces who conduct training and teaching of allied troops as part of their day-to-day operations. For Vietnam, the Coast Guard was once again called upon to ensure that South Vietnamese ports were safe from attack, using thirty 82-foot cutters to help secure the coastal areas. Coast Guardsmen also were assigned to the 37th Aerospace Rescue and Recovery Squadron, and lost one pilot killed in action while trying to evacuate American troops under fire.

As part of Desert Storm in 1991, the Coast Guard helped to secure the perilous Persian Gulf, working side by side with the U.S. Navy. It was also active in the Adriatic in support of the U.N. peacekeeping efforts in Bosnia and Kosovo.

Keep in mind that between each of these conflicts the domestic task of enforcing maritime safety and security never slackened its tempo, as boating grew in popularity in the United States, drug traffickers streamed into our southeastern waters, and storms and disasters continued unabated. And at each of these junctures of high-risk and complicated operations, the U.S. Coast Guard has added to its reputation as a dependable hybrid: a law-enforcement and public safety entity under the Department of Transportation during peacetime; and a valuable asset with proven sea-keeping abilities in wartime. As an underfunded civilian force, or as the fifth and smallest of the armed services, they have suffered from budgetary and manpower constraints. Yet the unique job they do, and the deadly competency with which they accomplish it, has never changed. One tenth the size of the navy, they nevertheless have more experience with hostile boardings—often after tracking down fast drug boats—and SAR—responding to one thousand distress signals a week—than any other service.

Responsible for saving thousands of lives and billions of dollars worth of property, the Coast Guard is poised to use its extensive experience and unique capabilities in the war on terrorism, as well as performing its "day job" of acting as our maritime police and life savers. Sometimes likened to a Swiss Army Knife, Secretary of State Colin Powell has called the Coast Guard a "unique instrument in the nation's national security tool bag."

One Day in November

Among the thousands of rescue missions the U.S. Coast Guard has performed, a recent example allows one to appreciate some of the abilities of this service. On November 24, 1997, a distress call was received from an Air Force jet. An F-15 of the 94th Fighter Squadron was reported down in the ocean seventy miles off the Virginia coast, and the weather was bad, with high winds and fifteen to twenty foot seas. With freezing water temperatures and an unpromising forecast, rapid response was the only hope for the pilot. Air Force pilots are equipped with a rubber raft that inflates when the pilot lands with his parachute in the water, but someone would have to get to the scene quickly.

The distress call was routed through an SAR coordination center, and soon a complex matrix of help was airborne and on the way. A U.S. Navy SAR helicopter was dispatched from an aircraft carrier at sea, and a Coast Guard HC-130 was launched from Cape Elizabeth, North Carolina. But the navy chopper was too far away, and the C-130 couldn't land on the water. A Coast Guard HH-60J Jayhawk helicopter was on the taxiway at Cape Elizabeth, its mission that morning to fly to Wilmington, South Carolina, to monitor an oil-spill clean-up. But in less than ten minutes the crew had changed their flight plan, loaded a rescue swimmer and his gear on board, and were charging over the stormy Atlantic to find the Air Force pilot.

They flew the eighty miles from their base to the crash site in thirty minutes and began to look for a white smoke flare dropped by the C-130. But they were unable to sight it due to the wind and waves. By then a Navy F-14 Tomcat had joined the rescue and was able to keep the downed pilot in sight while vectoring the Coast Guard chopper to within a quarter of a mile. There they sighted the green dye marker that the downed pilot had released in the water. The Coast Guard rescue swimmer was lowered forty feet from the hovering Jayhawk into the churning ocean, and he managed to get the pilot into the basket. But because of the waves, the cable attaching the basket to the chopper was going slack and threatened to wrap around one of the pilot's legs. Gingerly working the hoist, the basket was pulled up, only to have it blow underneath the helicopter. Finally the pilot was recovered into the cabin and placed inside a device like a sleeping bag designed to warm victims of hypothermia, the potentially deadly lowering of body temperature that afflicts those who find themselves in the North Atlantic in a November storm. Then the basket was lowered again to recover the rescue swimmer, and the helicopter took off at top speed for a hospital. The pilot made a full recovery.

In this relatively simple scenario some of the essential features of the Coast Guard come through clearly: its ability to respond instantly to accidents far off the coast; use of its own fixed-wing and rotary aviation assets; its easy interaction with the air force and navy; and its ability to deploy highly-trained and supremely fit rescue swimmers directly into the ocean to effect the saving of a life. When time was of the essence, with a worsening weather picture and already rough waters, the brave SAR experts of the Coast Guard, working closely with other armed services, were able to accomplish an extraordinary feat because of their experience and training, not to mention courage.

An HH-65 Dolphin helicopter performs a rescue demonstration in the Gulf of Mexico in September 2000. The young woman has volunteered to experience a "day in the life" of a Coast Guard rescue swimmer at Air Station Houston. (Dept. of Defense)

And the thing to remember is that they stand ready to do these kinds of missions every day and night of the year, in peacetime and in war.

Rescue Swimmers

While the navy has a mandated two SAR swimmers per capital ship, the Coast Guard has pioneered the concept of an individual acting as a crucial bridge between its helicopters and victims in the water. This was prompted by the tragic loss of the ship *Marine Electric* off the coast of Virginia in 1983, in which thirty-one of a crew of thirty-four perished. Although Coast Guard and Navy helicopters responded, most of the crew was too cold to load themselves into the rescue baskets that were lowered to them. After this accident it was determined that a new breed of rescuer was needed, one who would leave the safety of the helicopter and plunge into the surf next to the victim. One would think that finding such people would be difficult, but the Coast Guard found them and trained them.

To start with, there is an eight-week basic training at Cape May, New Jersey, during which physical fitness and the ability to respond to (and overcome) pressure is assessed. Suitable candidates then go on to a sixteen to eighteen week AST (Aviation Survival Technician) course held in Mobile, Alabama, where they fine-tune their skills while exploring the rigors of dealing with victims in all sea states and conditions. Equivalent to some Special Operations Forces standards, recruits are asked to be able to do forty-two push-ups in two minutes, fifty sit-ups in two minutes, five pull-ups, a one-and-a-half-mile run in less than twelve minutes, and a 500-yard swim in less than twelve minutes. They also need to be able to swim twenty-five yards underwater, four times in a row, with a minute's rest between swims. Rescue swimmers are also trained as EMTs (Emergency Medical

Technicians) and as helicopter crewmen. EMTs are the vital link between accident recovery and hospital care, and are trained in every phase of injury and illness, from heart attacks to head wounds, and are often the difference between life and death for victims. Forty to fifty new ASTs are trained and certified each year.

This training allows the Coast Guard to deploy men and women in top physical condition who are able to act decisively and quickly for up to thirty minutes in any sea state, down in the water with the people they are rescuing. Their training does not cover SCUBA operations, and they are forbidden from entering sunken vessels, but they do have masks and snorkels. If the situation warrants it, they are prepared to jump from a height of up to fifty feet into the swells, and the drill for that is to use the left hand to keep the mask on their face, right arm across their chest, and legs together with flippers pointed up so they won't hinder entry into the water. If the sea temperature is above fifty-five degrees, they use a standard wet suit; below fifty-five, a dry suit is substituted, which is a somewhat bulky garment that keeps the frigid water away from the skin of the rescue swimmer.

One of their many specialties is dealing with parachutes and harnesses, with which it is easy to become entangled in the water. They train with all the standard air force and navy pilot's harnesses, and can undo any strap or restraining clasp in a second. During their training they perform these tasks in pools and open waters with debris all around and in the dark, so that they won't become distracted when the real deal hits. There is a monthly fitness test to ensure that they are maintaining the high physical standards needed for the job, and medical training is ongoing for the duration of their service. Some rescue swimmers go on to become paramedics, but the majority are EMTs, which is adequate for most of their rescue tasks.

As in all aviation operations throughout the services, the pilot is in charge and makes the call about when and where to deploy the rescue swimmer, because they have command and responsibility for the helicopter and its crew at all times. If a rescue basket is lowered and the line becomes entangled on a wreck, it may have to be jettisoned for safety, as nothing will pull a chopper out of the sky quicker than being tethered to a bobbing boat. And fuel is always a consideration in offshore operations. In one case, after a pilot was rescued off the Oregon coast, the helicopter had to leave its rescue swimmer behind in bad weather. It scooted for the shore, landed, got the pilot into an ambulance, hastily refueled and hustled back to the place where the GPS said their AST was last seen. Fortunately, the rescue swimmer was right where they'd left her, floating in the Pacific.

Ships and Aviation Assets

To understand where the Coast Guard might fit into a Special Operations role, it's important to get a feel for the assets they now possess. There are three cutter classes—the largest ships the Coast Guard deploys—and unfortunately they are all getting old. This is rather a theme with USCG equipment, because while they consistently get high marks for their management of diminishing monies, their budget has gone down while their job load has gone up. The 378-foot Hamilton class is their largest, and is able to patrol anywhere in the world. Then there is the 270-foot Famous class, also elderly. Next is the 210-foot Reliance class, which lacks sonar and hangars for helicopters. Also, the diesel engine used in the Reliance class has only one other application in the world, and that is as part of a South African railroad. These vessels also lack either the Link-11 or Link-16 systems, which would enable them to have real-time voice, video, and data communication with navy ships. Unbelievably, the Coast Guard also lacks night vision goggles and satellite phone systems, and the top speeds of these cutters in no way approaches some of the "go fast" boats that drug runners favor. The USCG has had some success with using helicopters to run down these fast smuggling craft, but it is clear that they will have to be updated in the near future. The Coast Guard has always lacked strong advocates in government, partly because of the curious system by which they are part of the Department of Transportation during peacetime (since 1967), and are then transferred to the navy once the shooting starts.

There are a number of icebreakers and "aid to navigation" ships deployed by the USCG, but their 110-foot Island class patrol boats are a much more tactical and updateable platform. Everything under sixty-five feet is a "boat" (not a cutter or ship), and that's where you'll find the Motor Life Boats (MLBs) such as the 47-foot MLB which is designed to operate in bad weather and can right itself if overturned in eight seconds. Then there are the little boats, such as the Rigid Hull Inflatable, which has a deep-v hull of fiberglass and an inflatable collar all the way around the outside, making it a versatile and sturdy small boat. The 25-foot Transportable Port Security Boat has mountings for machine guns and grenade launchers fore and aft, and the 38-foot Deployable Pursuit Boat (DPB) is a high-speed (forty knot) answer to some of the "go fast" boats that are favored along our southeastern border by lawbreakers. Any of these might come into play for boarding parties and port security, as they are rugged and swift vessels that can move quickly and hit hard if armed properly.

Coast Guard boarding parties harken back to the days when naval ships would come alongside an enemy and send a small group over the rail to capture an opponent by small arms and courage. Today's boarding parties are fully armed with M-16s

A Polar Class 399 icebreaker, the largest cutter in the Coast Guard. These ships have reinforced hulls and special icebreaking bows, and a system that allows raid shifting of ballast to increase their momentum. (Coast Guard)

The 47-foot Motor Lifeboat is the Coast Guard's first response resource in high seas and heavy weather environments. Virtually unsinkable in the roughest conditions, they are designed to self-right themselves if capsized. (Coast Guard)

The 38-foot Deployable Pursuit Boat is the Coast Guard's craft of choice to intercept or pursue fast drug-running boats in the Caribbean and Eastern Pacific. (Coast Guard)

and Winchester or Mossberg shotguns, as well as the Beretta M-92, 9mm pistol with a fifteen-round clip. They are fully authorized to make arrests, or simply issue safety warnings if your life jackets and engine compartment are not up to snuff. Boarding is one of the most hazardous jobs that the Coast Guard does on a regular basis, and the manner in which the boardings are done has been commended by some, while it's earned some gripes from fishermen on the West Coast who tend to get boarded out of proportion to their illegality. Be that as it may, there is no better way to get a feel for a boat than to send a boarding party over their rails to inspect the ship and crew up close.

The USCG has four aviation assets at its disposal at this writing, a total of between 190 and 210 helicopters and airplanes depending on maintenance schedules. The long-range option is the sturdy and reliable HC-130 Hercules (a C-130 variant), whose four engines and known abilities have been useful world wide in every phase of military transportation and civilian cargo work. They are robust and steady planes that can land and take off on relatively short fields, and are much beloved by the pilots who fly them. For medium-range and faster response, the Coast Guard uses its twenty HU-25 Guardian jets, twin-engine planes much akin to commuter jets. With high speed and the ability to get above weather, they can often be the first on the scene of any trouble. (An additional seventeen HU-25s are in storage awaiting a budget for maintenance.) The two helicopter types are the HH-65 Dolphin, a short-range platform, and the HH-60 Jayhawk, which deploys rescue swimmers. None of these aircraft can land on the water, and none of them are as yet armed.

To put these assets in context, forty of the seventy navies of the world are "coast guards," and of those forty the USCG is 39th in terms of the modernity of its vessels. But in just the past six months the U.S. Navy has begun to bring Coast Guard crews aboard their Cyclone class PCs (Patrol Craft), and these fast and lethal ships may be transferred to the Coast Guard entirely. At 170 feet and able to do forty knots, the Cyclones are thoroughly modern Special Operations craft that previously supported Navy SEAL operations. They have two 25mm automatic cannons fore and aft with a range of 2,700 yards, grenade launchers, .50-caliber machine guns, and the latest in GPS and radar gear. At 330 tons, drawing a mere 7.8 feet in draft, they are a perfect stopgap between the 270-foot cutters and the 110-foot Island class cutters and the smaller Motor Life Boats (which are not armed). Smaller craft can be launched from the stern of Cyclones, meaning they can deliver commando teams close to shore much more easily than the vast majority of navy ships. And with their firepower and speed they can perform missions similar to the World War II PT boats, which caused such havoc in the Pacific among Japanese shipping by their reliance on speed, stealth, surprise, and a lot of guns.

Although they are not usually considered Special Operations Forces by their military brethren, members of the U.S. Coast Guard seem poised to take on a number of tasks that would be familiar to Special Operations planners and historians. These include their already enviable record in SAR and CSAR (Combat Search & Rescue); their role as both a law enforcement and combat arm of the federal government; their tasks overseas where the presence of a coast guard is less threatening than that of a navy; and the crucial job of port security for the continental United States.

And here is where their job gets really tricky. Now that we've extended our fishing boundaries to two hundred miles offshore from twelve miles, the Coast Guard's total area of responsibility has increased to 3.3 million square miles. Add to that the 360 ports that it is charged to protect, the 95,000 miles of coastline

The Coast Guard cutter Mustang *participates in Northern Edge 2002, Alaska's largest annual military exercise, involving all military services and reservists. The scenario here is that the tugboat has been taken over by terrorists aiming to disrupt the Trans-Alaska pipeline on shore.*

(including the Great Lakes), their response to oil spills, aircraft crashes (such as Flight 800 off the coast of Long Island and the recovery effort for John F. Kennedy Jr.), drug interdiction, boat lifts from South and Central American countries, overseas duties from the Adriatic to the Persian Gulf to the Philippines, flood disasters in the United States, and the need to defend ships like the USS *Cole* from small boats laden with explosives, and you have a sea service that is going to either transform or go under, and cannot afford to do the latter. The entire USCG budget of almost $4 billion per year is less than the cost of one aircraft carrier. Yet since September 11, 2001, the Coast Guard has performed 25,000 patrols of American ports, 450 boardings, 800 SAR missions, and responded to 95 cases of environmental pollution. While their budget has been cut and their manpower is the same as in 1967, the men and women of the U.S. Coast Guard have gone about their business in the finest tradition of "quiet professionals."

They have been tasked as guardians against not just storms and wrecks, but terrorists and enemies of all stripes. Nobody has yet hijacked an oil tanker and steered it into New York or Baltimore, although diabolical schemes of that nature may already be on terrorists' drawing boards. But if such a plan can be stopped, it will likely be as a result of a Coast Guard patrol spotting them, and a combined Navy SEAL/Coast Guard boarding party. And, as anyone who has studied them will be able to tell you, the dedicated personnel of the USCG will be, as they have ever been, "semper paratus." Always ready.

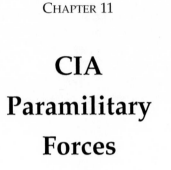

CHAPTER 11

CIA Paramilitary Forces

*I*n the world of Special Operations Forces, there is a sliding scale of units, from those whose men and equipment are well known and much photographed, all the way to groups of men who lurk in the shadows and keep a very low profile. Rangers, Special Forces, and Navy SEALs are easily recognizable by their bases, headgear, and insignia. But the covert warriors of the Central Intelligence Agency have always preferred to operate in the dark. Their missions are sometimes closely linked to those of more conventional Special Operations, but the details of their training, as well as the missions themselves, are lost in a mist of rumors and lies.

All of the standard military skills are part of their tool kit, from sabotage to ambushes, from land navigation to explosives. They are shooters and door kickers like their Delta colleagues; parachute qualified and SCUBA trained like Marine Force Recon and SEALs; adept at a range of communication systems and infiltration methods like Air Force SpecOps; and accustomed to working with indigenous peoples like their Green Beret brethren.

Yet they often operate in a twilight world of treachery and danger, where no man is their friend and the only hope for getting home is to think (and perhaps shoot) their way out of situations that would frighten any reasonable person to death.

The paramilitary (PM) capabilities of the CIA have also been the subject of much thought, discussion, and criticism, not only for their actions, but for their very existence. Intelligence agencies are supposed to receive their orders from the president, and then carefully gather and sift information from a staggering variety of places, including Open Source (newspapers, scholarly tracts, casual conversations), HUMINT (Human Intelligence, meaning agents whom CIA officers "run" or control as they gather information), SATINT (Satellite Intelligence, the eyes in the sky that currently fill much of the heavens), electronic intercepts from phones and computers, "walk ins" (those enemies who offer their services but may also be double agents bent on skewing matters), and any other resource that can be utilized.

Having gathered as much reliable information as possible given time and manpower constraints, the intelligence services are supposed to sift and discard, connect the dots and come back with valuable background information and recommendations as to how things should be played in the arena of diplomatic and military action. But there is another part of the CIA that exists far from the tweedy spies who troll for information throughout the world. The Directorate of Operations is the branch of the CIA that actually puts their thumb on the scale and goes out in the field to change things around by using military skills to accomplish a broad spectrum of tasks. These range from bolstering insurgent groups who oppose our enemies, to actual assassinations (in the bad old days and maybe again before too long), as well as mounting attacks on targets that have not fallen within the scope of Special Operations Command. As you might imagine, there is considerable debate as to the utility and long-term effectiveness of sending men into the field who behave in violent, unaccountable, and often unscrupulous ways under the heading of both "plausible deniability" and "in the national interest."

Be that as it may, there have been literally thousands of PM operations run over the years, and while they sometimes seem to present a long and twisted tale of tactics and tampering, there can be no denying that among the Special Operations Forces community they have blazed some of the brightest paths to glory.

History

As with so many SpecOps initiatives, the British led the way in PM operations with their SOE (Special Operations Executive) during World War II. This was a small group of men and women who received training in sabotage and clandestine military skills and who were then parachuted into the Nazis's Fortress Europe. They were often able to link up with resistance units, but these were also riddled with informers, making it better for teams to operate on their own if they could. Rightly judged to be spies, SOE members were tortured and executed if caught by the Gestapo.

As the United States came closer to being drawn into the conflicts that raged through Europe and the Pacific, one of the true giants in American history stepped forward to found the Office of Strategic Services, the OSS. William "Wild Bill" Donovan was a rare innovator whose restless energy and wealth of ideas led him to play a major role in not only organizing the United States's PM abilities during World War II, but also led directly to the formation of the CIA in 1947. A socially adept attorney, originally from Buffalo, New York, Donovan had fought in World War I as an officer and then commander of the legendary 69th Regiment, the "Fighting Irish," whose members also included

*William J. ("Wild Bill")
Donovan, founder of the
World War II OSS,
which in 1947 became
the CIA.*
(Library of Congress)

the poet Joyce Kilmer and the revered Catholic priest, Father Duffy. Donovan led them through some very hard fighting, and was awarded the Medal of Honor for his actions in the field in France, after leading his men despite serious wounds amid a withering hail of fire.

After the war Donovan started a law practice in New York City while keeping his social and political connections intact. With America's entry into World War II imminent, he proposed to President Franklin Roosevelt the creation of a governmental entity that could not only gather intelligence but also take a hand in fighting clandestinely wherever the need arose, from the Balkans to Burma. Roosevelt's advisors and top men like J. Edgar Hoover disliked the Irish lawyer and his idea, but the president saw the value of his concept and soon, driven by Donovan's dynamic spirit, men were being trained and sent off on dangerous missions behind enemy lines. Working closely with the British, especially Sir William Stephenson, American agents were sent to places like "Camp X" on the northern shore of Lake Ontario, where they were introduced to such skills as silencing outpost guards and sabotaging trains, and given rigorous training in hand-to-hand fighting. One exercise required them to talk their way into a Canadian power plant and place a block that represented an explosive device. Legend has it that one of the top graduates of Camp X was Ian Fleming, the British naval commander who went on to write the James Bond novels in the 1950s and 60s. The young men of the OSS proved to be quick and deadly pupils.

OSS operatives increased the tempo of their training after Japan bombed Pearl Harbor in December 1941, and PM assets were in place a year later when the Americans invaded North Africa. Often the OSS would infiltrate an enemy-held country to identify resistance groups, and arrange for them to be armed and trained so that they could effectively harry German and Japanese forces behind their own lines. The OSS sent men into China and Korea, as well as Burma and Indochina, where they found men who were leading grassroots resistance against the Japanese. Providing leadership and arms to the rag-tag forces, the OSS helped the locals wage classic guerilla warfare: a game of small numbers against a large occupying force. The trick was to strike the enemy on your own terms and at a time and a place of your choosing, so that you could have much greater impact than numbers alone would provide.

In Europe, "Jedburgh" teams were formed in England and parachuted into the embattled continent to sow havoc among the occupying Nazis. Men like William Colby (later to be Director of Central Intelligence after having run the Vietnamese operations of the Agency) were trained as paratroopers and saboteurs, operating in occupied Norway, Holland, and France under conditions of staggering danger. While the flashy parts of their jobs were against military targets, there was also a component of intelligence gathering and psychological warfare in their program. These multi-tasking special soldiers were paving the way for the postwar rise of the CIA, especially its operations division. Having launched successful missions on every continent except South America and the Antarctic, the OSS was disbanded at the end of World War II and Donovan was put to pasture. Or so it was thought.

Missions

The National Security Act of 1947 has a curious rider, making provision for "certain other actions," and it is on this slender reed that the legality of covert warfare rests. With the creation of the CIA in that year came an acknowledgment that the Cold War was fully underway and in deadly earnest, and that an array of innovative techniques would be used against Communist aggression wherever it was encountered. At first a number of operations were planned using native troops, from China to Hungary, as well as a few CIA contractors who would accompany them to disrupt the repressive regimes behind the Bamboo and Iron Curtains. Many of these early missions, however, were compromised and quickly caught, with the men being either executed on the spot or thrown into hellacious prisons for decades. One early operation was the training of Tibetans in Colorado who were then dropped back into their home country to fight the Red Chinese. CIA officers also helped the Dalai Lama to escape his occupied homeland in a daring trans-Himalayan march through high passes.

During the Korean War, CIA PM forces assisted the U.S. Eighth Army with its "White Tiger" initiative, which involved both amphibious assaults on Communist North Korea, and also groups of native dissidents conducting raids and ambushes behind the lines. It was expensive and dangerous work, but it was responsible for great damage to Communist logistics and the deaths of thousands of North Koreans.

The first great triumph of the CIA in paramilitary operations came when their agents were able to return the Shah of Iran to his hereditary throne in 1954. By infiltrating the country and hiring hundreds of dissidents, the CIA ran a huge deception and disruption campaign, conjuring riots where it was helpful to them, and attacking remote outposts in the barren countryside. The famous Frank Wisner was in charge of the Directorate of Operations in those days, and he used numerous OSS veterans for all manner of quasi-military thrusts against the Communists in Europe, South America, and Asia. With the full blessing of Allen Dulles, who was then the Director of Central Intelligence (DCI), paramilitary operations became an integral part of the foreign policy of the United States, providing arms and leadership to dozens of small groups.

At the same time a curious airline company got its start. The name kept changing over the years, including such innocuous sounding titles as Southern Air Transport, until it eventually came to be known as Air America. At one time it was the most successful airline in the world, with assets scattered from Europe and the United States to any number of small Asian countries. It kept establishing routes and buying airplanes, as its profit-and-loss ledgers were of no great concern. Air America was the CIA's private airline, and employed many of the wildest and best pilots who had ever flown a plane into a dense jungle airstrip. Using DC-3s and little Cessnas, Air America would go on to become a legend, especially in Southeast Asia.

In 1961, before most Americans could even find Laos on a map, a man named Tony Poe was in the country as a paramilitary officer of the CIA. Poe had enlisted during World War II, been wounded twice fighting the Japanese on Iwo Jima, and had then joined the fledgling CIA. He had gone through the standard training, including a psychological evaluation. During this, the shrink told Poe he had twenty minutes to compose a one-act play, which he was to act out when the doctor returned. When he came back, Poe exploded with obscenities, accusing the doctor of all manner of unspeakable transgressions, such as being a "pinko commie," and he finished by opening the desk drawer and hurling a pair of pink panties at the astonished medico. Supposedly he had talked the secretary into loaning him the compromising garments, and he passed the test by virtue of his ability to think quickly and do the unexpected. Unfortunately for Poe, the years to come would involve not only a torrent of combat and sacrifice for his country, but a career that would lead him straight into the heart of darkness.

As America's effort in South Vietnam began to gather steam in the 1960s, CIA paramilitary officers began entering the country along with Green Berets, both units keen to organize local peoples into a guerilla force that could hinder the Vietnamese Communists. Ironically, the Communists were led by Ho Chi Minh, who had once been armed and trained by the OSS. After victory over the Japanese, he had gone on to expel the French from Indochina, and was now threatening to take over the

American-allied South. Small groups of PM officers were busy setting up systems to arm and train the South Vietnamese and lead them in small excursions against the Communists.

Men like Tony Poe became fully immersed in the culture of Indochina, learning the language and sometimes taking native wives. (A rumor has it that Poe was the model for Colonel Kurtz in the movie "Apocalypse Now.") Poe had what was essentially a private army ten thousand strong which he led against the Communist Pathet Lao and their North Vietnamese supporters all through Laos. They fought every kind of action, from hit-and-run raids to full-scale pitched battles, and all of it was done outside the media glare that focused on the war in Vietnam. Using Air America for both transport and close air support, an endless war was waged in the shadows.

From this era comes the "cowboy" reputation of the CIA's PM efforts, because not only were there a few officers who wore blue jeans, six shooters, and Stetson hats, but also because of the reckless and often unaccountable nature of their operations. Because the war "over the fence" in Laos and Cambodia was secret, many of these campaigns and battles were conducted on a "need to know" basis, which didn't include the American public or the vast majority of their leaders. Regular U.S. forces were also sometimes used, as in the B-52 air strikes that were called in on enemy forces in Laos and Cambodia. The CIA paramilitary officers were among the bravest and most underappreciated of all our Special Operations Forces, and many of them fell in battle in godforsaken little jungle clearings, or in explosive plane crashes among the misty mountains of a forgotten land.

As the Cold War heated up, PM units also operated in Africa and South America, where they were able to capture and execute inconvenient left-leaning leaders like Patrice Lamumba in Kenya and Che Guevara in Bolivia. In all of these scenarios there was the same challenge: to go into a foreign land as a plausibly deniable asset of the United States, make contact with local allies, and arm, train, and lead native forces against the Communists. And whatever one thinks about the morality of their actions or the long-term effectiveness of PM operations, one has to respect the men who supported our fight in a hundred hellholes on every continent, and not for medals or good pay or because the work

Meo tribesmen crowd around an Air America helicopter during the evacuation of the Plain of Jars, Laos in March 1970. Later, during the fall of South Vietnam, Air America filled in the gaps of the evacuation by flying behind enemy lines to retrieve refugees and personnel. (AP)

223

was safe and easy. They went because they were volunteers in a desperate struggle, were able to operate in places where we didn't want to deploy the Marines or Airborne, and they were able to fight like blazes with whatever was at hand.

As the war in Vietnam built to epic proportions, so did the secret war "over the fence." The men who were being recruited now were mostly ex-military, because the Green Berets, Marine Recon, and Ranger LRRPs (Long Range Reconnaissance Patrols) were the men who had the most pertinent training and experience, and had learned to operate in the jungles almost as well as the natives. When the United States withdrew from Vietnam, a few guys like Tony Poe stayed behind, fighting on despite the fact that their government had declared the war a lost cause.

CIA PM forces were next spotted in the dirty war in Angola, fighting side by side with a hodgepodge of mercenaries and hired guns, countering the Soviet-backed Cuban expeditionary force. There was also an effort to clean up the secret warriors, spurred by the Church Committee hearings in 1975 that revealed many previously unknown episodes, such as the CIA's involvement in the failed Bay of Pigs invasion of Cuba. In that operation PM officers armed and trained Cuban exiles and even put together a rag-tag air force. The failure of that mission led to the dismissal of Allen Dulles by President Kennedy, and re-evaluation of the ways and means of conducting covert operations. There were also questions about Air America's involvement with the opium trade in Laos and Cambodia, and surprise at some of the assassinations and failed assassinations, such as the abortive attempts to kill Fidel Castro. Whatever free hand the CIA paramilitary forces had previously been given to pursue SpecOps work in the shadows was seriously reeled in. But not for long.

With William Casey as DCI under Ronald Reagan, the whole circus cranked back up as CIA officers went into Central America

Cuban leader Fidel Castro jumps from a tank during the Bay of Pigs operation in April 1961. The CIA-organized invasion by Cuban exiles was decisively defeated by Communist forces. (AP/Bohemia Magazine)

to fight in Nicaragua and Panama, using SCUBA gear to mine harbors, and helping to arm and lead the Contra rebels in a secret war run by Marine Colonel Oliver North of the National Security Council. North's imaginative funding efforts—secretly selling arms to Iran so that the Iranians would fund secret U.S. operations in Central America, with Congress none the wiser—led to a scandal that almost toppled the presidency. But Ronald Reagan shrugged his way through, genuinely perplexed why anyone would consider America resisting Communism in the Western Hemisphere a scandal. And in the end all was forgiven by the next president, George H. W. Bush (a former DCI), who declared with a straight face that he had not been "in the loop." These years saw a consolidation of PM in the CIA, and a bit less of the "cowboy" ethos of the Vietnam and Angola years. Estimates indicate that the paramilitary forces of the CIA never grew beyond five hundred or so men (and now, for the first time, women), but those people who were operating in Lebanon, Somalia, Iraq, and other hot spots were a new breed. They continued to be mostly ex-SpecOps forces, but there was a little more accountability, sometimes to the point where operations were called off by desk-bound bureaucrats far from the action.

The Reagan years also brought extensive CIA operations in support of the Mujahideen, the Afghan Muslims who fought the Soviet Union and ultimately defeated them, hastening the end of the Communist empire. In yet another ironic twist of the PM world, Osama bin Laden was one of the resistance fighters who received our help in the struggle against the Russians. CIA operatives vied with Pakistani intelligence during those years over which Mujahideen groups should receive the most aid. The United States favored the moderate parties while Pakistan preferred the Muslim fundamentalists. After the war the Pakistanis would help put in place the most radical group of them all, the Taliban.

Under President Clinton during the 1990s, the paramilitary forces deployed throughout the world against a new enemy, Muslim terrorists, while they also tried to secure the nuclear arsenal of the former Soviet Union. Following Desert Storm in 1991, it is said that CIA PM officers were among the U.N.-sanctioned inspectors who were allowed into Iraq, where they helped to organize such desperate ventures as the 1996 failed coup against Saddam Hussein. They continued to fight and die in relative anonymity, although for the first time books began coming out exposing the secret side of the war in Vietnam. The Directorate of Operations also underwent a name change, now being called the Special Activities Division, as if it was responsible for planning surprise parties or promotional events. Keep in mind that the PM efforts of the CIA are just one facet of the many things our intelligence agencies do every day, and that the electronic intercepts and satellite recon photos of the NSA (National Security Agency) were coming to play an ever-larger role, often completely replacing the old-fashioned HUMINT and PM operations. Many felt this was to the detriment of our efforts, and that a reliance on desk jockeys and computers was leaving us open to attacks from abroad, as was indeed the case in September 2001.

The CIA's paramilitary forces were among the first U.S. personnel deployed to Afghanistan after the World Trade attacks, and they suffered the first U.S. combat fatality of the war when an officer, Johnny Michael Spann, was killed while interviewing prisoners. For the first time, a shadow warrior was hailed as a hero mere days after his death, instead of years later. Spann would get one of the formerly anonymous stars carved into a block of Vermont marble at CIA headquarters in Langley, Virginia. They commemorate fallen CIA officers and not a few of those stars represent the sacrifice and fighting spirit of the CIA's paramilitary. The secret warriors had come out of the closet, and

A prototype of the RQ-1 Predator robot aircraft. With a 49-foot wingspan it can stay in the air for forty hours, providing real-time video of the ground. These CIA-run craft were introduced to the war in Afghanistan in fall 2001, armed with Hellfire missiles. They are "flown" by real pilots looking at a video screen instead of through the cockpit window.

were in hot pursuit of America's enemies. Estimates tell us that the CIA had twenty to thirty officers in their Near East Division who had strategic alliances and experience with the Northern Alliance, with whom they had been working since 1997, as well as PM officers who had participated in the war against the Soviets years before.

Training

Many of the CIA's paramilitary officers today come from the ranks of Special Forces and elite units such as the Navy SEALs, Marine Recon, Green Berets, Airborne Rangers, and Air Force Pararescue Jumpers (PJs). Our government has already spent thousands of dollars to train each of these men, and their experience and maturity are much appreciated in dire circumstances. They are mostly already Airborne qualified, many have language skills, probably have seen some combat, can shoot and march and navigate and sleep and live in wild country, and have that quiet and laconic special strength that seems to be imbued in all Special Forces operatives. As such they make fine PM officers.

For those coming in from the civilian world, the CIA runs job fairs at colleges and has a good website (complete with a kid's page), and there is still a little of the "old boy network" out there, where a friend might ask you out for a drink and propose that you serve your country in a "special way." They like recruits to be American citizens under the age of thirty-five and without a lot of legal, financial, or mental complications. For those who pass the rigorous screening needed for a security clearance, there are numerous physical and psychological evaluations. Polygraph testing and a complete background check may be followed in six to ten months by an invitation to report for training, and that's about where the evidence trail stops. What we do know is that the CIA has a main training facility at Camp Perry near Fall's Church, Virginia, which is known as "The Farm." It's been there since the 1950s, and consists of beautiful rolling horse country with deep woods and some hills. There the course selection is reputed to include "Flaps and Seals" (opening envelopes secretly), lock-picking, hand-to-hand combat, courses on the structure of U.S. intelligence agencies and the history of the CIA, exercises involving the intricacies of following people through the streets of Washington, DC, and likewise how to thwart someone following you, the proper use of safe houses and communication gear, some shooting, the use of "dead drops" (secret places in public where messages may be left and retrieved), wiretaps and computer surveillance, how to recruit and run an agent, and probably a warning not to think of themselves as James Bond or Matt Helm. If they carry around a lot of secret cameras and invisible ink or try to use their shoe for a phone, they may risk a reprimand.

For those going on to paramilitary operations, Airborne training (or refresher) will be next, followed by a thorough indoctrination with every commercially available firearm in the world, the ins and outs of guerilla warfare, how to make friends with primitive and not-so-primitive peoples, how to call in air strikes, and how to survive on the run in a hostile country. For that there are any number of fine governmental facilities, such as the U.S. Navy SERE (Survival, Evasion, Resistance and Escape) school just west of Stratton, Maine, and Point Harvey in North Carolina, which has its own airstrip and as many creeks and inlets as anyone could want. They also learn how to fly, drive, and steal any boat, plane, truck, or car they may happen to require.

Each step of the way they are trained to think on their own and operate in a world that threatens treachery and danger at every turn. Sleeping in the same place every night is dangerous. Having a set routine is a death sentence. Being paranoid is not something to be avoided, but just another factor to work with. After all, people really are trying to kill them. As a PM officer one can count on a life of secrecy, utilizing every aspect of the full Special Operations Forces arsenal but without a nice uniform or much hope of recognition—just the knowledge that they volunteered for a dangerous job that had the highest value to their country, and one that only a paramilitary officer could pull off.

In normal times it is estimated that the CIA's PM establishment is about 150 men and women, including pilots and support staff. There's no way to tell what those numbers are now, but there can be little doubt that a number of recently retired Special Forces personnel received a discreet phone call in the weeks after September 11. The paramilitary forces of the Special Activities Division answer only to the president and the NSC, and as such they are at the spear's tip when America needs to project power abroad quickly, quietly and with decisive results.

CHAPTER 12

Weapons, Equipment, and Transportation

*E*very occupation has its tools of the trade, be it the editor's red pencil, the carpenter's robust hammer, or the archaeologist's ground-penetrating radar. Special Operations Forces are no different. To get their jobs done they often need to carry an astonishing array of weapons and gear, only limited by how much a person can carry over distance in a hurry. When the load gets to be too much, there are a number of ways to transport gear, up to and including antitank weapons, from All Terrain Vehicles to helicopters and the Mark V SEAL Delivery Craft. The range of Special Forces weapons and gear is staggering, from the lowly chemical glow stick to the most sophisticated night vision and satellite navigation and communication devices, but they all have to pass a few tests: the weight test, the water test, the drop test, and the "Boy I wish I had a..." test.

Edged Weapons

Knives are one of the oldest and handiest tools on the planet: simple, quick, and silent. When things need to be cut in a hurry, as they often do in life, there's nothing quite like cold steel. The trusty knife is as much a badge of Special Operations Forces as any bit of gear, being featured on a number of unit patches.

The ancient Egyptians buried iron and bronze knives in their pyramids, and the obsidian blades of the Aztecs proved able to pierce rib cages without effort; but today there are many more choices. Special Forces troops have carried and used the three most famous knives in history: the Bowie Knife, the K-Bar, and the Sykes-Fairbairn Commando Knife, as well as the ubiquitous folding knife and some interesting variations on edged weapons. The Bowie is a cumbersome but awesome weapon, with its broad blade and double-edged tip, but it weighs a lot and isn't very delicate for fine cutting tasks. The K-Bar is a combat Bowie with the same general blade shape, and first won renown in World War II as the official issue USMC fighting knife, as well as providing a smaller version as a survival knife for Army Air Corps and Navy forces. The Sykes-Fairbairn is a World War II British development that is slender and double edged.

Knife fighting is taught as a skill to enable the removal of lone sentries on dark rainy nights at remote outposts, but soldiers report that in the field the knife is mainly used to prepare meals and perform minor medical procedures. Be that as it may, Special Forces men like to have knives around, and they like to have them strapped upside down on their left chest where they can be drawn quickly. Knife throwing is considered a suitable way to waste time between deployments, but the idea of throwing your weapon away in combat is viewed with disdain.

Machetes are used to break trail in heavy brush and jungle, and can also be quite lethal if swung hard enough. Russian Spetsnaz are reputed to be deadly wielding the entrenching tool with a sharpened edge, and are even trained to throw their shovels great distances, but this style hasn't caught on in the United

States. Being stubborn colonials at heart, when U.S. forces need-ed a weapon a bit more provocative than a knife or a machete in Vietnam they returned to their roots and reintroduced the toma-hawk, which terrified British troops during the Revolution and is still as lethal as it was then. Some concepts never go out of style. The Vietnam tomahawks had a slender head with a cutting sur-face on one side and a diamond-shaped spike on the rear.

The basic double-edged knife with a blade between six and ten inches long is still the standard, although recently there has been some interest in the traditional Japanese-style Tanto blade, which is single edged and has a sharply defined point for punch-ing through body armor. Modern knife sheaths have come a long way since the arts-and-crafts days of leatherwork, and today they are most often made of ballistic Kevlar, and always feature a retaining snap to keep the blade in the sheath, especially when carried upside down. Knives can also be worn in the boot top, on a forearm, in the small of the back and just over the right shoul-der mounted on a pack.

Folding knives have seen a tremendous development in the past twenty years, and such companies as Spyderco and Gerber have produced blades that can be carried safely and securely folded and clipped onto gear or in a pocket, and then deployed with one hand, the thumb being used to snap the blade out where it is locked in place by a fairly strong locking mechanism. Some of these knives have amazing abilities, like the Spyderco, which can saw through metal (such as a tin can or an automobile roof). Folding multi-tools like the Leatherman also have a SpecOps application, being like Swiss Army Knives on steroids. Few soldiers will have occasion to use all the doodads to be found in the handles of these versatile tools, but when you need a Phillips screwdriver, for example, your K-Bar or Tanto isn't going to do.

Traditional Weapons

While they are not standard issue, many SOF troopers know how to make and use a variety of traditional weapons such as spears, bows and arrows, crossbows, and slingshots. These might be improvised in a survival or escape mode, and provide a weapon when there is no other option. The spear is a handy extension of a sharp point (such as your knife secured to the end of a pole), and can be used to fish or kill things at a slight distance. The bow and arrow is an ancient system for extending your lethal reach, and a fairly good bow can be made in a morning. The modern crossbow is a devastating device that shoots bolts out to one hundred yards or so, and has impressive shock and stopping power. And the slingshot is a quiet and fast way to hurl a projectile at considerable speed. The modern Wrist Rocket type is potentially lethal with ball bearings. Trained as they are to "adapt and overcome," it shouldn't be surprising that Special Operations Forces are very hard to completely disarm, and can revert to primitive weapons quickly and easily if they have to.

Pistols

Pistols are carried in the field as an option of last resort. Because of their limited range and accuracy, and their lack of barrel length and magazine capacity, they are hardly considered serious combat weapons. But they do come into use in the world of SpecOps for a number of tasks, such as hostage rescue. The M1911 Colt .45 Automatic was the standard sidearm of the United States for almost a century, and for good reason. It is a massively slab-sided and robust pistol with a seven-shot clip of short, fat bullets that will knock down almost anything it is aimed at, including hostile forces and wild pigs. It is hard to teach people to shoot with it accurately, because it makes one hell of a bang and flash and the recoil alone causes most gentle stay-at-home folk to flinch and miss their target. Gunsmiths do fine-tune Colts for target work, but the standard issue pistol has the general feel of a sledgehammer, and about the same effectiveness. Be that as it may, the Colt has built itself such a reputation that it is still to be found in holsters where the wearer feels the need of a slug that will stop whatever it hits in a hurry and mostly without a lot of fuss. One difficulty of the Colt as a SpecOps tool is that it is considered to be unwise to walk around with a round in the chamber, even with the safety on and the hammer down. Therefore, to use it quickly means that you have to draw the pistol, rack back the slide to cock it and place a shell in the chamber, take the safety off and then acquire your target.

The M-9 Model 92F Beretta solves many of the problems of the Colt, and for that reason it was selected as the new standard issue U.S. sidearm. It has a magazine capacity that is double that of the Colt, and can be carried safely with a round in the chamber, meaning that your combat drill with the Beretta is simply to draw the weapon, take the safety off, and fire. The trigger is able to initiate the first shot, after which recoil starts the slide working and away you go. The Beretta is also more comfortable to hold and, as a 9mm, somewhat easier to teach soldiers to shoot with. It is a forgiving pistol, and target acquisition after a shot is considerably easier than with the Colt. It can be fitted with a silencer that reduces the noise to a semi-loud "thwup!"

The Mercedes-Benz of modern pistols are the Glock and the Sig-Sauer, Austrian and Swiss automatics of high magazine capacity and flawless workmanship. One Glock was buried in sea sand at the shore for two weeks and then dug up and fired immediately. One shudders to think of trying this with a Colt .45. These are both expensive pistols, and what you get for your money are accurate and wonderfully built handguns that will pass every test thrown at them, while also being solid and easy to maintain.

But what of the lowly revolver? It still has its place, especially the new lightweight .357 Magnum (such as the legendary handguns of Smith & Wesson), which is a powerful round in a tidy carrying package. The best feature of a revolver is that it doesn't jam: if you get a bad round, simply pull the trigger again and the cylinder will revolve and bring you what is hopefully a better one. With an automatic, a bad round means a jam in the system, and just as with a computer printer, that means a pause while you clear the jam by racking the slide and getting the thing ready to go again. These pauses are deemed unwise in combat. As long as there are rounds in the cylinder and the cylinder keeps going around, there will be metal and flame coming out of the front of a revolver. This also brings up one major drawback of revolvers: they mostly have a five or six shot capacity, and can be slow to refill even with speed reloaders.

Pistols are carried on the right hip, often slung low, or under the left arm in a shoulder holster, and modern holsters have a side pocket for a spare magazine. Silencers are cumbersome and wear out after just so many shots, but may be used to quietly shoot a sentry, or, as in the case of the silenced .22s and Smith & Wesson automatics of the Vietnam era, against guard dogs (the so-called "hush puppy").

Submachine Guns

Submachine guns are light weapons that fire fully automatically, meaning you can empty the clip if you just keep pressure on the trigger. They are not known for their accuracy, but are easy to carry and can sling a lot of lead in a hurry, making them great for the point man on a patrol or for hostage rescue. But automatic fire makes the weapon shake and the muzzle climb, meaning that a lot of training has to be put into making users fire accurately. Learning to "snatch" at the trigger and firing short bursts are ways to compensate for the muzzle climb.

The familiar Thompson submachine gun (M1928, M1 and M1A1) is a fairly heavy gun that fires from a drum or a clip, using the same ammunition as the Colt M1911, the .45 Colt Auto round. It shares the same knockdown capability as the Colt pistol, but is surprisingly complicated and fussy about its care and feeding. It was replaced with the M-3 .45, the "Grease Gun," which was a General Motors product made out of stamped metal much the same as some of the cheaper cars. As such it was cheap and easy

An airborne gunner and his loader on maneuvers. The problem of carrying ammunition for guns that fire 1,000 rounds a minute may soon be solved with the army's adoption of a "robot mule," which will tag behind a squad guided by sensors. The mule is scheduled to enter service in 2008. (Dept. of Defense)

The MP-5 submachine gun is a favorite of Special Operations Forces that expect close-in combat. Compact and lightweight, it can also be fitted with a sound suppressor. (U.S. Army)

to build, although it had a tendency to jam because of a feed problem. The 9mm Uzi of Israeli manufacture was one of the first successful small submachine guns, with its magazine mounted inside the hand grip, making it balance well and enabling one handed (not very accurate) fire for the flamboyant user.

Today's Special Forces carry the 9mm Heckler & Koch MP-5, a beautifully designed and made submachine gun that is short and accurate, making it perfect for confined spaces such as "Killing Houses" and inside helicopters and personnel carriers. The HK MP-5 has swept the field in submachine guns, and this clever company just keeps improving their fine product as time goes on, making better silencers, laser sights and flashlights built into the weapon, all manner of folding stocks, and absolutely bombproof reliability. Two or even three magazines can be lashed together making a fresh supply of 9mm near at hand. Delta Force and the CIA paramilitary forces have access to an MP-5 that fits in a briefcase, with the cocking lever and trigger in the handle, making for a prosaic-looking bit of luggage that can spew death unexpectedly in formal business environments.

Assault Rifles

The M-16 was a quantum leap in assault rifles, known as the "plastic rifle" because of its reliance on new polymers to replace the old wood and steel construction methods of the past. When the M-16 was first issued in the 1960s there were some problems with maintenance and jamming in the wet and muddy conditions of Vietnam, but enforced care for the weapon by the users and a redesigned magazine feed cleared most of that up. The M-16 fires a .223 bullet that is no ordinary diminutive rim fire .22, but instead a high-speed military bullet with fantastic stopping power. They have been used to saw down small trees.

The modern version of the M-16 is the same 5.56mm (.223), still made by Colt, and is called the M-4A1. It is a shorter and lighter improved version of the well-tested M-16, and can also carry an M-203 40mm grenade launcher or a 12-gauge combat shotgun with a separate barrel under the main rifle barrel. These are very handy little weapons that still have a great deal of range, and come with a lot of options such as a collapsible butt stock and provisions for single shot, 3-round bursts (another way to defeat muzzle climb) and fully automatic fire. This rifle is an interesting case of a Special Operations Forces weapon becoming the new standard-issue rifle for the rest of the armed forces.

The M-16A2 incorporates the latest improvements in the M-16 series of rifles. It can be selected to fire single shots or in 3-round bursts. (U.S. Army)

A Navy SEAL stationed in Kuwait fires an M-4 carbine fixed with an M-203 grenade launcher. Sharing ammo with the M-16, the compact M-4 is often preferred for Special Operations.

The British have been using a bull pup design for a decade now, where the magazine is behind the trigger, which enables it to have a long barrel for accuracy and yet still retain a short overall length, but the idea has not caught on in the United States. There are also new designs with "caseless" ammunition being touted around the world, but it seems as if the replacement for the M-4A1 will be a Heckler & Koch design, building on their peerless reputation.

Shotguns are still an important part of the SOF arsenal, especially for soldiers walking point on patrols and for door-

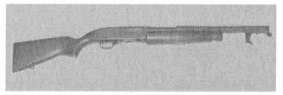

kicking or other close-quarters actions. This 12-gauge pump shotgun has a 7-round tubular magazine and can be fixed with a bayonet. (U.S. Army)

Shotguns

SpecOps units sometimes carry a traditional pump action shotgun, such as the 12-gauge Winchester or Mossberg, and these are still among the best ways to respond to walking into an ambush, boarding a hostile vessel, or knocking in the door of a terrorist safe house. The psychological impact of a shotgun begins with the large hole at the business end of the barrel, and extends to the unique sound of the slide being worked to place a shell in the chamber. Shotguns are short range and therefore relatively safe to use around non-targets such as civilians, in the hands of a good shooter, and high impact, firing a variety of munitions from bean bags for non-lethal encounters to Double Ought pellets (each about the size of a .38 bullet) and even slugs, which are just really large bullets. They tend to shred their targets but, like the Colt .45, shotguns have a reputation of stopping problems before they get out of hand, sometimes just by working the slide.

SAW

The Squad Automatic Weapon (SAW) is a clever Belgian design that replaces the old M-60, which replaced the heavy Browning Automatic Rifle of World War II and Korea. The idea is

The M-249 is the Army's latest light machine gun, smaller and more compact than the M-60, allowing the gunner to carry more ammunition. (U.S. Army)

to provide each squad with its very own machine gun, and the need has changed little since the BAR was designed at the end of World War I. The SAW is an automatic weapon heavier than the M-4 carbine, that can also fire longer bursts, and can use either its own see-through box of ammunition or the standard M-16 rifle clip, being the same caliber (5.56mm). It also makes a good weapon for the man at the front, or for defending a position when a lot of bullets is going to be better than a few good shots. Known as the M-249, it also has a big brother, the M-240, which is 7.62 caliber and weighs in at twenty-four pounds.

Sniper Rifles

Sniping is as old as the introduction of gunpowder, and has often been viewed with loathing by its victims, and with great delight by its practitioners. Special Forces snipers operate in two-man teams, a shooter and a spotter, and once they stealthily place themselves in range of an enemy, they begin by shooting the officers (spotted by their binoculars and lack of rifle and rucksack) and radio operators (who often have an antenna attached to a large backpack), thus taking out the leadership and communications of an opposing force. Once the brains and voice are eliminated, all but the most professional enemy will commence to dissolve or go around in circles.

The M-24 Sniper Weapon System is based on the venerable Remington 700, a well-tested and much-loved hunting rifle. It is bolt operated and fires a Winchester .300 Magnum round out to about five hundred meters. The caliber is changed to 7.62x51mm when used in conjunction with NATO forces, but has much the same abilities. With a five-shot magazine and Kevlar construction, this is a state-of-the-art shooting system, and can be used with either its iron sights or a 10X scope. Snipers go through intense training to enable them to stalk and kill their prey, and must be comprehensively versed in woodcraft and patience to set up and make their kills, often after a lengthy waiting period.

The Barrett .50

This amazing rifle, in experienced hands, can place a large bullet accurately onto a target at a range of almost one mile. The lack of recoil and noise and flash are significant, as is the effect of the M-82A1. You don't hear it coming, you just die. They were first used in Operation Desert Storm to attack Scud missiles and their operators behind Iraqi lines, and the system has been worked on since then to provide better recoil suppression and advanced sights. This semi-automatic rifle will continue to provide sniper capabilities that can take out helicopters, light vehicles, fuel dumps, and anyone in their area.

Grenades

Modern grenades are smaller than their World War II antecedents, but pack more punch and are easier to throw. The M-67 fragmentation grenade is easily stowed in a pocket, and three or four may be carried, perhaps two fragmentation and two smoke. Grenades also come in a range of flavors, from shrapnel to different colors of smoke (used for signaling to air crews or artillery observers) to tear gas to white phosphorous (WP) that

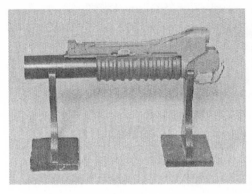

The M-203 40mm grenade launcher is designed to fit under the muzzle of an M-16A2 rifle. (U.S. Army)

burns at about 1,500 degrees even underwater. Also issued to certain SpecOps Forces are "flash bangs," which are all noise and light, meant to deafen and blind bad guys in hostage situations just long enough for the good guys to shoot all the non-hostages dead. These concussion grenades can also be used as booby traps and perimeter warning devices, as can any of the others. Grenades all have a pin and an arming lever that is often taped down. To use one the pin is pulled and the arming lever is allowed to fly away. It is then hurled as far as possible. (The factory setting on the fuse is about five seconds.) To use as a booby trap, the pin is taken out but the arming lever is kept with the grenade, such as by putting it in a small can, and the grenade is tied to a trip wire. When the grenade is pulled out of the can, the arming lever flies off and lots of mayhem follows.

Communications

Hearing and being heard is even more important in combat than in ordinary life. Without their radios SpecOps troops are at great risk of wandering into barrages and being unable to act as the eyes and ears of higher commands, rendering them heavily armed tourists in a combat zone. For this reason they use up to seven different radios and systems for calling home, and bring along spare parts when they can. But there are all-in-one packages. For long-range talk, the standard issue is the AN/PSC-5 (V) made by Raytheon. It has the ability to work both in UHF and VHF modes, as well as line-of-sight and satellite communications. Weighing in at about twenty pounds with its battery, the PSC-5 is the answer to the old radioman's dream—a lightweight and network-ready small package that can talk all the way back to McDill and Washington if need be. One radio for every four to six men is a good SOF average. These radios can be used with an earpiece and in whisper mode for stealthy missions, and can also transmit coded messages in bursts that are very hard to trace, intercept, or jam.

Navigation

Navigation and route finding are the essential skills of military units, and SpecOps guys are among the savviest users of all the many tools a navigator has at his disposal. The standard military compass has a tritium lighting system and is light and tough. Global Positioning is also used to get around and designate targets for air strikes and artillery; but they work on 9-volt or AAA batteries, which always fail when you need them the most. It is a very foolish person who carries a GPS unit and just hopes for the best. Special Operations Forces hope for the best, but they plan for the worst. If need be they can always revert to the standard topographical map and compass, and count their paces with astonishing accuracy to find where they are within a very tight range. One of the tests in Ranger training is to indicate your present position to the instructor using not your thumb or forefinger or a wave of your hand, but with a single pine needle. For that kind of accuracy you need to very carefully monitor your pace, and use deft landscape analysis to determine just exactly where you might be. And this also applies to night missions and over incredibly broken terrain like ravines and steep valleys. Special Forces are also adept at matching up satellite photos to maps, and using any type of map that may fall into their hands (including nautical charts) to make their way into (and out of) danger.

The Ranger counting beads are a good example of low-tech that works. These are two sets of beads on a leather or parachute cord. They simply measure their average stride over a mile, and then count their steps in the field. When they get to one hundred, they slide down a bead. When they do ten of those they slide down one of the other beads, enabling them to pretty accurately (with practice) tell how far they've gone, adjusting for steepness of terrain.

Land Vehicles

Any ride will do in a pinch, but Special Operations Forces like to have their own dedicated wheels when they need to tear around the landscape. Dirt bikes and All Terrain Vehicles have been used with great success, as have snowmobiles and the lowly pick-up truck. (The Taliban seemed to prefer Toyotas for their driving needs. The "Buy American!" campaign never really got off the ground there.) But the ride of choice is the Humvee (in the desert called the Dumvee), that weaponized SUV that AMC began making fifteen years ago, and that General Motors has now taken over. This astounding rig can drive through puddles that would sink your BMW X5, climb walls and go over ditches, take a good pounding from small arms and yet remain a stable and reliable platform. It can also have all sorts of rocket launchers and machine guns attached.

The High Mobility Multi-purpose Wheeled Vehicle, commonly known as the Humvee, is the modern descendant of the military jeep. When used in the desert in Iraq, SOF troops nicknamed them Dumvees.

Aircraft

The C-130 has got to be the poster child of Special Forces, having as many roles as there are missions, doing everything from acting as a simple transport to belching fire in the form of the AC-130 Spectre gunship (manufacturers suggested retail around $72 million). With its 25mm Gatling gun, its 40mm Bofors, and the 105mm howitzer, there's hardly anything that can stand up to it, or would do so willingly. The old Hercules has been updated numerous times, but the basics remain: four sturdy Allison turboprop engines, short take-off and landing, handy rear ramp, massive empanage (tail), and robust and redundant lines for the essential fluid that moves all the control surfaces. The MC-130 Combat Talon is the platform for inserting and extracting Special Forces, and it's going to be a while before they find a better plane than this Boeing superstar and all of its variants. Command and Control, transport, gunship, and rugged ride home, the pilots who fly these don't miss being fighter jockeys. They've got their very own world of excitement.

The UH-60 Black Hawk is still the Army's mainstay helicopter for air assault or general support. As this photo reveals, the jeep hasn't entirely disappeared from the U.S. TOEs. (U.S. Army)

The world's most devastating close-air-support weapon, the AC-130 Spectre gunship bristles on its port side with miniguns and howitzers. The pilot circles above the target while computer-coordinated fire can put holes into every square foot of a football field-sized area within seconds. (U.S. Army)

The AH-6 Little Bird was specially designed for SOF operations. Light and versatile, it can land in an urban street as easily as a desert, or as in the case of Operation Urgent Fury, on top of a Panamanian prison.

For helicopters, Special Operations Forces uses the elderly but beloved and mighty twin rotor MH-47E Chinook, some of which can land on water and deploy rubber rafts (made by Zodiac and known as "rubber ducks"), as well as carrying forty-plus men and all their gear to altitudes of up to 15,000 feet. There is also the Pave Low, an updated H-53, and the new Pave Hawk. The Pave Low is a big helicopter that can carry thirty-plus men and their gear, and has a crew of six, many of whom can operate the machine guns and miniguns mounted on the sides and even shoot out of the back ramp. The Pave Hawk is a somewhat smaller chopper based on the Black Hawk, which is now the most famous chopper in the world thanks to the loss of a couple and a certain magnificent book and movie. For in-close operations, say in alleyways, the Boeing H-6 series Little Birds provide versatility, advanced avionics, and a six-barreled mini-gun.

With the on-again-off-again nature of the CV-22 Osprey—a tilt-rotor hybrid that seems to be unstable and dangerous despite the fudging of safety records—Special Operations Forces will have to rethink how they move men and gear around the land-

An HH-60 Pave Hawk performs a sea extraction. These long-range (refuelable) craft are cousins to the UH-60 Black Hawk. (U.S. Air Force)

scape, whether that means extending the life of its already ancient flying platforms, or else the emergence of some new design that can get the job done in the new century. The jury is still out on the future of SOF helicopters.

The easiest way to get in and out of these aircraft is to find the right one on the landing strip and show your ticket before stepping on board. But it's never that easy. They can also parachute out of them, fast rope down to the ground, rappel down, use a rope ladder (which is very hard if someone isn't holding and stabilizing the other end), or just jump if it's not more than say twenty feet. That's into water. For coming back aboard it's great if the pilot can land, but often they cannot or are unwilling to loiter on the ground, and for that they can use the hoist and steel cable on the side, or else hook up to the extraction rig which uses a special harness. Then they simply fly away with the soldier hanging off like the raccoon tail on a bicycle, and with about as much control over their flight. Hopefully they will land or reel them in before flying low through thorn bushes or into the middle of a thunderstorm. That's where their radio can help them make their wishes known.

Odds and Ends

Let's pause for a few kind words for the ordinary gallon Ziploc and standard industrial duct tape. These two wonder products of the modern age find much use in all phases of Special Operations, and indeed no person going outside can afford to be without as much of both as can be carried. Also in their rucksacks and pockets will be found parachute chord (with a very high breaking strength) and rubber bands for tying things down and keeping them where you put them. The gallon Ziploc is tight and waterproof, and they can use two of them doubled if what's in them is very important. Duct tape (also known as "100 mile an hour tape") is a perfectly ordinary product, but the good black industrial type is more useful than words can express. With it they can make instant repairs, fix a tent or a backpack, secure a prisoner, and even use it as low-rent wound dressing, at which it excels. It's not pretty, but like so many SOF items, it does the job, and that's the bottom line.

Chem Lights are plastic cylinders that can be stored for years. When they wish to have a steady glow without heat or sparks (good for working around explosives and fuel), they bend the wand in the middle until they hear a crack, and then shake it up. Eight to twelve hours of luminescence is the result, bright enough to hike with or signal a sharp-eyed observer, but very subtle. They can be strapped to a helmet so that someone can follow and work underwater just as well as in the air.

And don't forget a good watch—shockproof, waterproof, with illumination, and easy to read. Being on time is more than good manners in commando operations. SpecOps Forces tend to prefer black plastic or nylon straps, and it's hard to beat the Casio company for a tough watch that doesn't cost an arm.

Boots and Clothing

Because Special Operations Forces missions are so varied, the men doing them often have wide latitude to pick and choose the clothing they will need. This might include Nomex gloves and balaclava (which are flame retardent), jump boots or sneakers, issue BDUs or "deniable" camouflage patterns, and all manner of hats, helmets, berets, and ball caps. The army testing labs in Natick, Massachusetts, have been working very hard to bring the armed forces up to the minimum levels that outdoors enthusiasts have taken for granted for the better part of two decades, including such familiar items as fleece hats, neck gaiters, jackets and vests, polypro shirts and leggings, advanced wool/polypro

Night vision goggles are quickly becoming standard issue to U.S. soldiers, whether infantry, naval or aviation. Long gone are the days when Japanese night binoculars gave them an edge over the U.S., as at the naval Battle of Guadalcanal.

socks, Gore Tex gear that keeps water out while allowing perspiration to evaporate away from the skin, and clothing that doesn't rustle when you move. The Marine Corps has recently accepted the army's invention of Jungle-Desert Boots, which can simultaneously stop Punji sticks as well as keep the sand from between your toes. (The steel layer formerly inserted into jungle boots made them impractical for the desert, like walking on hot plates.) The British Royal Marines typically wear gaiters to keep rocks and moisture out of the top of their boots in difficult terrain, however the Americans view these odd garments with suspicion.

If it is occasionally hard to equip our most elite troops in a manner expected by the most casual weekend hiker, the explanation lies with the laborious procurement system, which recently prompted the chainstore Home Depot to prohibit its stores from selling anything to the government, due to the bewildering complexity of paperwork and restrictions that the government requires.

But there has recently appeared quite a light at the end of the tunnel. In May 2002 the Department of Defense unveiled a prototype called the Objective Force Warrior, which was a mannequin dressed in the uniform of the future. It eliminates annoying nightvision or infrared goggles, as well as cumbersome laser targeting devices or communications gear. All this is now in the helmet, which also features a visor that allows the soldier to see the big picture as if through two 17-inch computer screens. The uniform itself is equipped with thermal sensors that can measure a trooper's heart rate, body temperature, exposure to chemical or biological agents, and his daily calorie intake. Airflow will be regulated within the fabric to provide warmth or cool as the case may dictate. Even better, for heavy gear, each squad will be equipped with a "robot mule," guided by sensors, which can carry the ammo, water, heavy weapons, or souvenirs. As a scientist announced, "We have completely rebuilt the combat soldier as we know him." The Objective Force Warrior is expected to be available for the services in 2008.

CHAPTER 13

A Special Operations War: Afghanistan

The United States suffered the most devastating surprise attack in its history on September 11, 2001. Within a terrifying space of two hours, the towers of the World Trade Center, those soaring, 110-story symbols of American might, were struck one after another by hijacked airliners. Another jetliner crashed into the Pentagon and still another nosedived into the ground near Pittsburgh. As smoke and flames spewed over Manhattan, the World Trade towers suddenly collapsed, burying three thousand civilians under millions of tons of rubble. Among the dead were hundreds of heroic NYC firefighters and police who had rushed into the conflagration rather than away from it. Their job had been to save lives but instead they gave their own. In Pennsylvania, it was learned that Americans had tried to seize back their plane from the terrorists and their last words before rushing the cockpit had been "Let's roll." They too sacrificed their lives, aboard a jetliner that had turned around and was heading straight for Washington, DC. Those men may be the reason why today the White House still stands.

The nineteen hijackers involved in the September 11 attacks were quickly identified by U.S. Intelligence as members of Al Qaeda, a shadowy terrorist network first formed from Muslim veterans of the Soviet-Afghan War. Its leader was Osama bin Laden, a Saudi national, whose headquarters and base camps were now in Afghanistan. President George W. Bush addressed a shaken American public that evening. "We will make no distinction," he declared, "between the terrorists and those who harbor

While the World Trade Center smolders, a USAF Special Operations MH-53 helicopter from Hurlburt Field, Florida, stands guard against further attacks. (U.S. Air Force)

them." Afghanistan was controlled by the Taliban, a group that practiced an Islamic fundamentalism of medieval ferocity. In response to Bush's demands to hand over bin Laden, the Taliban leader, Mullah Mohammad Omar, refused. The United States was thus at war not only with shadowy terrorist cells sprinkled around the globe but with a nation that willingly supported them. Afghanistan—landlocked, mountainous, halfway around the world, and with a fearsome warlike reputation earned against foes from the ancient Greeks to the Soviets—was now in the crosshairs of the United States. And America's first war of the twenty-first century would be fought like no other in its past.

Bush's first correct step was to keep his hand off the Cruise missile button. During the 1990s the United States had relied on stand-off weapons as a quick panacea against terrorist attacks, accomplishing little except an increase in the enemy's confidence. This time, America calmly assembled its strength. The carriers *Enterprise* and *Carl Vinson* sailed with their naval battle groups for the Arabian Sea south of Afghanistan.The carrier *Kitty Hawk*, stripped for helicopters, set off from its base in Japan, and the huge nuclear carrier *Theodore Roosevelt* slipped out of Norfolk, Virginia. The U.S. Air Force began beefing up stocks of fuel and munitions at bases from Germany to Bahrain to Diego Garcia in the Indian Ocean.

But for troops on the ground the most important calls went out to Special Forces at Fort Bragg, the Rangers at Fort Benning, the Marines at Camp Pendleton, the 10th Mountain Division at Fort Drum, and to MacGill Air Force Base, Florida, the headquarters of SOCOM. In addition, over two thousand Coast Guard reservists were called up to protect America's shores. On September 20 President Bush addressed both houses of Congress and the nation with an eloquent call to arms. "We'll meet violence with patient justice," he said, "assured of the rightness of our cause and confident of the victories to come." He also said, "I've called the armed forces to alert." In fact, they were already on the move. This was to be a war fought by America's Special Operations Forces, supported by its rapid deployment elites. Together with U.S. air power they would achieve success sooner than anyone expected and veritably awe the world with America's new capacity to wage flexible, fast, unconventional war.

At this writing—on a day when a Special Forces camp in central Afghanistan has just been attacked—it is not possible to describe operations in full detail. (Nor should it be.) We still don't know exactly when U.S. SpecOps Forces penetrated Afghanistan (or how); and reports that Delta operators were already inside the country on September 27 wait verification. Nevertheless it is possible to describe events in broad detail, with special focus on the fact that while the Bush administration warned the American public of a "long, hard war," the deployment of Special Operations Forces caused the Taliban regime to fall like a house of cards in three months.

On October 7, 2001, after Bush had given the leaders of Afghanistan a final warning, America attacked from the air. The first strikes, from navy fighter-bombers and U.S. heavies, along with missiles fired from U.S. ships and a British submarine, destroyed the Taliban's air and air-defense capacity. Over the next two months, 4,700 combat sorties would follow until our airmen simply ran out of targets. Just as in Desert Storm, America appeared to be softening up its opponent with air power, while covert combat operations remained outside the public's view. But then the Pentagon released an astounding video of American troops staging raids in the heart of Taliban territory. The dramatic scenes taken through a nightvision lens showed Army Rangers and Special Forces operating near Kandahar. American troops were already far behind Taliban lines.

Secretary of Defense Donald Rumsfeld visiting Rangers at Fort Bragg, near Fayetteville, North Carolina, in November 2001. Rumsfeld gained a high appreciation for Special Operations Forces during the war in Afghanistan. At one point he told a crowd, "When the President dials 911, the phone rings here in Fayetteville." (Dept. of Defense)

The Rangers had made a low-level nocturnal parachute drop to secure an airfield south of the city. This would later turn into Camp Rhino when the Marines came ashore. Special Forces troops had invaded one of Mullah Omar's compounds. Encountering only light opposition, they ransacked the place, seizing documents and files that may have proven invaluable in the operations to come. Tragically, a Black Hawk helicopter following the mission in a CSAR role went down in Pakistan, both crewmen killed. The Special Forces and Rangers were meanwhile extricated seamlessly by copters dispatched from the U.S. fleet in the Arabian Sea. Five Special Forces troopers had been wounded in the operation at the compound while a number of Rangers were reportedly injured in the parachute drop. If the U.S. public was fascinated to see this first evidence of U.S. ground response to the September 11 attacks, the Taliban leadership was alarmed. Special Operations Forces had come in and out of their backyard at will.

The south of Afghanistan, where these raids took place, was the Taliban's home territory. They held more tenuously above the Hindu Kush, where the Northern Alliance had continued to resist Taliban rule. In the north, the Pentagon was not about to release footage of ongoing operations, but some details did come to light.

In early November a Night Stalker Pave Low helicopter flew for six hours on a black night to deliver its cargo: a Special Forces

Dusk on one of the first days of Operation Anaconda in Afghanistan. Note that the 10th Mountain troopers have not yet lowered their night vision goggles which will give them an advantage over Al Qaeda forces after dark. (U.S. Army)

A-Team of twelve men, accompanied by an Air Force SpecOps Combat Controller. The A-team was left off on a 6,000-foot mountain where icy winds chilled them to the bone and treacherous cliffs were only a footfall away. The team had been landed some ninety miles within Taliban territory.

After two days of marching up and down mountains with their heavy packs and no sleep, the A-team made contact with General Osta Atta Mohammed of the Northern Alliance. But then a new challenge arose. The Tajik general spoke Dari and neither he nor his men knew English. The A-team of the 5th Special Forces Group all spoke Arabic but that didn't work. They tried French, Spanish, German, Chinese, all with no dice. Finally a Special Forces trooper tried Russian, and bingo. One of the Afghans knew it and communications were opened.

The A-team took a look at the two thousand ragged, freezing Northern Alliance troops and their first act was to call in a U.S. airdrop of boots, clothing, blankets, and food. This established their prestige in the eyes of the Afghans, but even greater assistance was to follow. The A-team began to march with the Afghans toward Mazar-i-Sharif, the main Taliban-held city in the north. On the way they came to an enemy outpost in a village. The Special Forces painted it with lasers and called in U.S. airstrikes. The Northern Alliance troops practically jumped with glee when they saw their hated enemy blasted apart by 2,000-lb. bombs delivered by streaking jet fighters.

Just south of Mazar, the Tajik force met up with a force of Uzbeks led by the notorious warlord Rashid Dostum. The Uzbeks had been accompanied by a Special Forces A-team of their own. Another Northern Alliance force, this time of Hazaras (descendants of the Mongols) led by General Haji Mohaqiq, joined the force from its territory within the Hindu Kush. The U.S. public was amused at this time when pictures were released of American Special Forces troopers riding horseback across the northern Afghan plains together with Afghan cavalry. The combined contingents then mounted an assault on Mazar-i-Sharif. The Northern Alliance easily overran the airfield and then the city itself. To everyone's surprise, the Taliban collapsed, thousands of troops defecting to the Alliance. When entering the city, a Special Forces soldier recalled, "We were locked and loaded." But then he found himself surrounded by jubilant civilians, some of them weeping with joy. He said, "I wondered whether it was the same feeling the Allies had when they liberated Paris."

At the beginning of November the United States dispatched additional Special Forces and Ar Force Combat Controllers to assist and coordinate Northern Alliance troops. U.S. air strikes were delivered with ever-increasing accuracy, blowing apart Taliban positions thanks to laser guidance or GPS coordinates dispatched to the skies by operators on the ground. (Air Force SpecOps might have gone overboard by also dropping four 15,000-lb. "daisy cutter" bombs, which blow up everything across a square mile.) On November 13 Kabul fell almost as easily as Mazar-i-Sharif, the Taliban disintegrating or fleeing to the countryside. During that triumph, Special Forces troops, who had grown beards in order to be as inconspicuous as possible, stayed to the sidelines while the population cheered its Northern Alliance liberators. Nevertheless there was tension as different Afghan groups eyed the prospect of control of the capital, and 160 additional U.S. Special Forces operators and British commandos were flown in to keep order.

The last Taliban and Al Qaeda stronghold in the north, Kunduz, fell during the last week of November, but at the same time the United States suffered its first combat fatality. It was an officer of the CIA's Special Operations Directorate, who had been interviewing prisoners in a fortress at Mazar-i-Sharif. The Taliban prisoners had revolted and Johnny Michael Spann, a former Marine captain, was killed. His partner was able to escape while a full-fledged battle broke out. The Special Forces A-teams on the scene suffered five wounded (from a U.S. airstrike hitting too close to their position) while of the four hundred revolting prisoners, eighty survived to surrender. Among these was a twenty-year-old from California, John Walker Lindh, or "Jihad Johnny," as he has come to be known.

The 15th Marine Expeditionary Unit had meanwhile entered the country in the south in the longest helicopter insertion the Marines had ever undertaken, from the carriers *Peliliu* and *Bataan* five hundred miles away. On the first day, probing Cobra helicopters from the force destroyed an enemy vehicle convoy. Otherwise the Marines dug into their base at Camp Rhino south of Kandahar.

While the Taliban had only held tenuous control of Kabul and the north, its base territory was the mountainous east and the more flat south, centered on Kandahar. Special Forces A-teams were already in this territory, organizing resistance among Afghanistan's largest ethnic group, the Pashtuns. On December 5, four A-teams, who were guiding a Pashtun force led by future Afghan leader Hamid Karzai, were suddenly attacked by five hundred Taliban, speeding across the landscape from Kandahar in eighty machine-gun-mounted pick-up trucks. The Afghan resistance fighters began to panic but the Americans rallied them into a line before the village of Tarin Kot. The A-teams feared that if the village was left undefended the Taliban would wreak vengeance on the civilians. The operators called for air support, which arrived quickly and disrupted the Taliban attack. Then the Taliban dismounted and began to flank the Americans and Pashtuns on foot. The U.S. operators deployed their allies so that each flank was refused, while they kept up a disciplined fire. The Special Forces continued directing aircraft to pulverize the attackers. Tragically, one 2,000-lb. bomb landed on friendly lines, killing three members of the 5th SFG and six Afghans. Speculation was that at the height of the battle a trooper had mistakenly dispatched his own coordinates to a B-52, resulting in the errant bomb. Air Force and Army Combat Search and Rescue helicopters meanwhile came in to evacuate thirty wounded, nineteen of them Americans. Karzai had suffered a slight wound in the cheek.

Two days later, Kandahar was abandoned by the Taliban, the Pashtun warlord Abdul Qadir playing a major role in negotiating their withdrawal. (Qadir went on to become a vice president in the Karzai government but was assassinated in Kabul a few weeks later by unknown gunmen.) Taliban leader Mullah Omar may have been given a free pass to escape, as the fighting in Kandahar was waged between rival Pashtun groups seeking to replace his rule.

But with the Taliban on the run, America remained concerned with its primary antagonist, Osama bin Laden, whose cave complexes, established during the Soviet war, were in the east near the Pakistani border. Intelligence located him in a rugged patch of mountains called Tora Bora (Black Dust) and U.S. Special Forces and British SAS converged on the area, along with many Afghans who now appeared to be willing allies. The only failure in the campaign occurred in the first weeks of December when Afghans who offered to track bin Laden in the mountains provided misleading reports, claiming to have coaxed an Al Qaeda surrender and then to have killed hundreds of them among the heights. Their reports proved false as the Al Qaeda troops and their leader slipped across the border to Pakistan. That country's vow to "seal the border" was likewise unfulfilled. (Pakistani troops were historically loathe to venture into the tribal territories.) Afterward there was an unconfirmed report from the *London Spectator* that an SAS "Sabre team" had gotten a fix on bin Laden in Tora Bora but were refused permission to move in. The Americans wished to do the job themselves. Unlike the British, however, they were unfamiliar with the wiles of the locals. (Adding mystery to confusion, most of the U.S. Army Rangers had already been withdrawn from the theater, receiving a warm welcome back at Fort Benning on December 7.) In any event, bin Laden escaped.

The war had meanwhile produced a startling new airpower innovation in the Global Hawk, a high-altitude reconnaissance drone that was rushed from its development to participate, and in its lower-flying, more lethal relative, the RQ-1 Predator, which fired Hellfire missiles. These robot aircraft could fly for forty hours at a time, roaming the battle zone for prey while providing real-time video to commanders and controllers. Run by the CIA, these craft were "flown" by real pilots, the only difference being that the pilots looked at a video screen instead of outside a cockpit window.

On January 4 a Special Forces soldier was killed and an accompanying CIA officer wounded by feuding Pashtun in the eastern mountains. This event underscored the increasingly vague nature of the "lines" of the campaign. At the beginning of January the Marines were replaced at Camp Rhino by the Rakkasans, formally known as the 187th Regiment of the 101st Air Assault Division. And the Rakkasans arrived in the country looking for a fight. A Pashtun compound north of Kandahar took the brunt of their wrath in a devastating nocturnal raid. Twenty-one Afghans were killed and twenty-seven captured. The fly in the ointment was that the Afghans claimed they were not (or no longer) Taliban and the attack was launched due to faulty intelligence, most likely provided by rival Afghans. The Screaming Eagles remained fairly quiet for a month but at the beginning of March received another opportunity for combat.

In the nearly inaccessible mountains of eastern Afghanistan, which had been built-up during the Soviet war and which had always defied conquest, U.S. Intelligence identified a large pocket of remaining Taliban and Al Qaeda. Operation Anacondawas launched to erase the vipers' nest and this time, instead of relying on Afghan auxiliaries to lead the way, the Afghans would only probe while U.S. forces were airlifted into the mountains to provide blocking positions against enemy escape. The specific target was the Shah-i-Kot Valley southeast of Gardez. The 101st would coordinate with elements of the 10th Mountain Division to seal it off with main forces while U.S. SpecOps troops looked for opportunities in the valley.

The battle got off to a clumsy start when one of the Afghan columns attacking into the valley from the northwest ran into a torrent of fire and retreated. A Special Forces sergeant at the head of the column was killed. Inside Shah-i-Kot itself, all hell broke loose. A six-man SEAL team with an Air Force Combat Controller tried to land on a high ridge but their helicopter came under a barrage of RPGs and small arms. A hydraulic line burst, covering the floor of the cabin with slippery oil. Hovering ten feet off the ground, the Chinook was hit by another RPG that forced the pilot to jerk. One SEAL, Neil Roberts, went flying out the back hatch of the copter and another was dangling by his tether. (Roberts may have undone his own tether in order to help the other man.) The damaged craft managed to escape down the mountainside to rendezvous with a second copter. The SEALs, in the good copter, then went back to the ridge. When they disembarked they were again hit by enemy fire from all directions. The Air Force SpecOps officer was killed and two SEALs were wounded. The team decided to retreat down the mountain. By this time a Predator drone had arrived overhead to videotape events, sending back images to General Frank Hagenbeck of the 10th

Two Apache helicopters of the 101st escort a troop-carrying Chinook from Kabul to Kandahar. The troops aboard the Chinook were returning from Operation Mountain Lion, in which they had probed Afghanistan's eastern mountains alongside British Royal Marines in April 2002. (AP)

Mountain Division, who had designed the operation. It appeared that after falling to the ground, Roberts engaged in a one-man firefight against Al Qaeda, moving about the area engaging them with his SAW (Squad Automatic Weapon) for half an hour. At one point he knocked out an enemy machine-gun emplacement. But in the end three enemy fighters had walked up to his final position and dragged his inert body away. Earlier, Roberts had written to his wife how much he loved being a SEAL. "If I died doing something for the Teams," he wrote, "then I died doing what made me happy."

A platoon from Alpha Company, 1st Ranger Battalion, had meanwhile taken off from Bagram airbase to support the SEALs. They weren't aware that the SEAL team had gone back down the

267

mountain and that Roberts was gone, so they flew into the same hornets' nest. About a mile from the ridge, their Night Stalker helicopter was knocked out of the sky by enemy fire, bullets crisscrossing through the cockpit. The craft lurched to the ground and the Rangers piled out. One was killed while still in the copter and two more on the ramp. Everyone in the cockpit was wounded. Outside, the remaining Rangers fired back against the Taliban and Al Qaeda overlooking them from heights on both sides. During the seventeen hours they were pinned down, their Air Force CCT bled to death from wounds, because additional helicopters were refused permission to land. But F-15s and F-16s zoomed in, "danger close" no longer a consideration, and one of the enemy positions was obliterated just seventy-five yards away.

Troops from the 101st Air Assault and 10th Mountain Divisions were now engaged throughout the valley, sometimes landing into buzzsaws of enemy fire. At altitudes from 8,500 to 11,000 feet, the Americans dug in beneath barrages of mortar and RPG fire, enemy machine-gun and small-arms fire pouring into their positions. A 101st trooper was killed and dozens from both divisions wounded as they stubbornly held their ground, giving back in turn against the dug-in enemy. Soldiers often had the enemy in plain sight and could see the effect of their rounds. In this battle, Kevlar body armor earned its stripes. One 10th Mountain trooper was hit twice in the chest. Knocked down for a second, he jumped back up and resumed firing. Army Apache helicopters had soared in to provide close support but so many were shot up that the call went out for Marine Cobras, which flew in from the carrier *Bonhomme Richard*. Soon it was Al Qaeda that called it quits. Opposing fire died down as the enemy began fleeing the area. For the next week, U.S. aircraft pummeled the 60-square-mile valley. With B-52s up top, Predators, jet fighters, Spectre gunships, and ground-attack helicopters, the U.S. layered the sky above the battle zone. The operation had involved twelve hundred U.S. troops along with two hundred Special Operations Forces from Europe and Australia.

After Shah-i-Kot, the Taliban and Al Qaeda refused to stand in battle and their diehard remnants appeared to have drifted off to the wild tribal areas of Pakistan. In June, the Afghans held a loya jirga (grand council) that included sixteen hundred representatives from throughout the country. Hamid Karzai was reaffirmed as interim leader of the new government, pending free elections to be held within two years.

In July 2002, the 82nd Airborne Division arrived in Afghanistan to replace the Rakkasans of the 101st. "We've got it a whole lot better than the 101st," one trooper remarked, "because they built the tents we now have." Of course the 101st may have gotten the last laugh because after spending spring in the southern desert of Afghanistan, 82nd troopers inherited the brutal July and August. At this writing, army A-teams continue to probe central Afghanistan for remaining Taliban fighters, while army operators and CIA PMs have also been verified on the ground in Pakistan. There, if he is still alive, is bin Laden, whose death or capture is anticipated. FBI agents have also arrived in the theater. Their Hostage Rescue Teams are sometimes compared to Delta Force and SEAL Team Six as America's premier counterterrorist assets.

Of course no war would be complete without some friction between Special Operations Forces and the regular army. On May 31, Lieutenant General Dan McNeill replaced the 10th Mountain Division's General Frank Hagenback as commander of coalition forces in Afghanistan. Seeing that combat had died down and discipline had gotten lax, McNeill ordered the men to resume saluting officers. (Saluting is forbidden in a combat zone because it identifies officers to snipers.) The troops grudgingly

Civilian Mike Low examines a medallion and photo of his daughter, worn by Staff Sgt. Mark Baker of the Night Stalkers. Low's daughter was a stewardess on one of the planes that was hijacked and crashed into the World Trade Center on September 11, 2001. Sgt. Baker carried the medallion on over twenty missions in Afghanistan, in honor of Sarah Low. (AP/*Kentucky New Era*)

went along, except a sign popped up outside the part of Bagram airbase where Delta troopers were stationed. It read: "No Saluting Zone." McNeill caught wind of it and the next day the sign was torn down.

A Reflection on Operation Enduring Freedom

The American war in Afghanistan was an eye-opener, revealing the awesome, finely honed capabilities of our specialized warriors to the U.S. public and the world at large. While the Bush administration had constantly warned of a long, protracted war, U.S. Special Operations Forces, coordinating their efforts with our air force and naval air power, leveraged an amazingly quick victory. Prior to U.S. involvement, the Northern Alliance had been fighting the Taliban for six years. Once American operatives had entered the theater, the Taliban fell in nine weeks. (Army Special Forces A-teams hold the palm, and one hopes they will no longer bristle when the public returns to calling them by their more familiar name, the Green Berets.) The Rangers, Air Force SpecOps, the Marines, SEALs, Airborne troopers, 10th Mountain, CIA paramilitary and, back at home, the Coast Guard, which dispatched special port security units to guard the Al Qaeda POW camp at Guantanamo, all deserve kudos.

At the time Kabul fell, the Department of Defense stated that there were no more than three hundred U.S. ground troops in Afghanistan. But what a three hundred they were. These were our most skilled warriors, whose exact exploits will only eventually emerge as soldiers leave the service or are given clearance to describe the details of their insertions, combats, and travails. What we already know is that they engineered the campaign to quick success and the world now stands in awe of their achievements.

If there was any failure in the campaign, it came from U.S. political leaders who, despite the unspeakable carnage of September 11, remained weirdly reluctant to aggressively commit more troops to the battle. While Special Operations Forces were covertly inserted into the greatest danger behind enemy lines, an overt commitment of forces seemed almost taboo to the

271

Department of Defense. Some three hundred of our two thousand Rangers were sent to Afghanistan, two hundred of those returning to the States even before the battle at Tora Bora took place, the clash during which Osama bin Laden escaped. The Marine 15th and 26th MEUs did everything that was asked of them—in one case beating off a Taliban attack on Kandahar airport—but they could have done more. The 101st Air Assault Division was visibly annoyed at missing out on the main action while the 82nd Airborne was held back for ten months. This is not to mention the conventional forces of the U.S. military, every man and woman of which was anxious to contribute to the campaign after September 11.

The consequences of this hesitation can be measured not only in the escape of the Taliban and Al Qaeda leadership but in the current problems of the Karzai government, which is packed with ministers from the Northern Alliance—that ragtag force which formerly held only 10 percent of the country and which was led to victory by our SpecOps. The political resolution would have been better served if more American troops had been available to participate in the triumphal march through Kabul so that a firmer grip of the postwar would be in hand. As it stands, the American campaign, though executed in astounding fashion by our "quiet professionals," may come back to haunt us as the Afghans resume their age-old practice of civil war. The British have recently given up their leadership of the peacekeeping force, handing it over to the Turks. American troops, save roaming army A-teams, continue to be confined at Bagram and south of Kandahar. It is possible that a large enough American stamp wasn't impressed upon the country during the period when our moral authority alone was unassailable. More U.S. personnel, both from within SOCOM and the conventional forces, should have participated.

But not to quibble. Though on the ground American power was projected by a mere few, those few set an example of astounding skill and courage. Dropped into dark freezing heights half a world away, surrounded by enemy forces, and charged with the leadership of disparate allies, our specialized forces exceeded all expectations. Afghanistan was, above all else, a Special Operations war. A worry is that U.S. political leaders will get entirely too comfortable with only putting SOFs in "harm's way." But a greater feeling is pride that in the recent war our elite forces vindicated their training and their long history, and have only opened a new door to their future potential.

Appendix

Tables of Organization

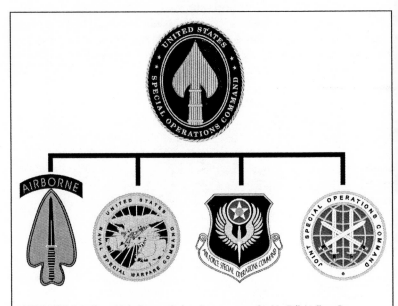

USSOCOM, formally established as a unified combatant command at MacDill Air Force Base, Florida, on April 16, 1987, is commanded by a four-star flag or general officer with the title of commander in chief, U.S. Special Operations Command (USCINCSOC). All SOF of the Army, Navy, and Air Force, based in the United States, were eventually placed under USCINCSOC's combatant command. USSOCOM's three service component commands are the Army Special Operations Command, the Naval Special Warfare Command, and the Air Force Special Operations Command. The Joint Special Operations Command is a sub-unified command of USCINCSOC.

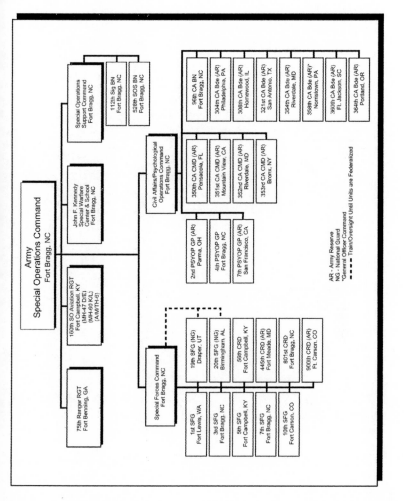

975

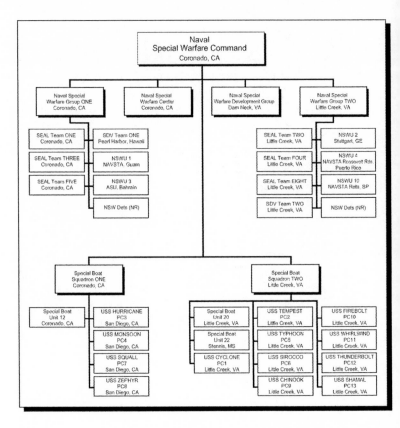

Air Force Special Operations Command
Hurlburt Field, FL

919th Special Operations Wing (AFR)
Duke Field, FL
- 5th Special Operations SQ (AFR)(MC-130P) Duke Field, FL
- 711th Special Operations SQ (AFR)(MC-130E) Duke Field, FL

18th Flight Test Squadron
Hurlburt Field, FL

AFSOC Air Support Operations Squadron
Ft. Bragg, NC

16th Special Operations Wing
Hurlburt Field, FL
- 4th Special Operations SQ (AC-130U) Hurlburt Field, FL
- 6th Special Operations SQ (Aviation FID, UH1) Hurlburt Field, FL
- 8th Special Operations SQ (MC-130E) Hurlburt Field, FL
- 9th Special Operations SQ (MC-130P) Eglin AFB, FL
- 15th Special Operations SQ (MC-130H) Hurlburt Field, FL
- 16th Special Operations SQ (AC-130H) Hurlburt Field, FL
- 19th Special Operations SQ (TRNG) Hurlburt Field, FL
- 20th Special Operations SQ (MH-53J) Hurlburt Field, FL

193rd Special Operations Wing (ANG)(EC-130E)
Harrisburg IAP, PA

USAF Special Operations School
Hurlburt Field, FL
- 10th Combat Weather SQ Hurlburt Field, FL
- 21st Special Tactics SQ Pope AFB, NC
- 22nd Special Tactics SQ McChord AFB, WA

720th Special Tactics Group
Hurlburt Field, FL
- 23rd Special Tactics SQ Hurlburt Field, FL
- 24th Special Tactics SQ Ft. Bragg, NC

352nd Special Operations Group
RAF Mildenhall, UK
- 7th Special Operations SQ (MC-130H) RAF Mildenhall, UK
- 21st Special Operations SQ (MH-53J) RAF Mildenhall, UK
- 67th Special Operations SQ (MC-130P) RAF Mildenhall, UK
- 321st Special Tactics SQ RAF Mildenhall, UK

353rd Special Operations Group
Kadena AB, Japan
- 1st Special Operations SQ (MC-130H) Kadena AB, Japan
- 17th Special Operations SQ (MC-130P) Kadena AB, Japan
- 31st Special Operations SQ (MH-53J) Osan AB, Korea
- 320th Special Tactics SQ Kadena AB, Japan

AFR - Air Force Reserve
ANG - Air National Guard

277

Select Bibliography

Bank, Col. Aaron. *From OSS to Green Berets: The Birth of Special Forces*. Novato, California: Presidio Press, 1986.

Beckwith, Col. Chas. A. *Delta Force: The Army's Elite Counterterrorist Unit*. New York: Avon Books, 2000.

Bohrer, David. *America's Special Forces: Weapons, Missions, Training*. Osceola, WI: Motorbooks International, 1998.

Bohrer, David. *America's Special Forces: SEALs, Green Berets, Rangers, USAF Special Ops, Marine Force Recon*. St. Paul, MN: MBI Publishing Co., 2002.

Bonds, Ray (ed.). *America's Special Forces: The Organization, Men, Weapons, and the Actions of the United States Special Operations Forces*. Miami: Salamander Books, 2001.

Brehm, Jack and Pete Nelson. *That Others May Live*. New York: Crown Publishers, 2000.

Cerasini, Marc. *The U.S. Special Ops Forces*. Indianapolis: Alpha Books, 2002.

Clancy, Tom, with John Gresham. *Special Forces: A Guided Tour of U.S. Army Special Forces*. New York: Berkley Books, 2001.

Clancy, Tom, with Gen. Carl Stiner and Tony Koltz. *Shadow Warriors: Inside the Special Forces*. New York: G.P. Putnam's Sons, 2002.

Eshel, David. *The U.S. Rapid Deployment Forces*. New York: ARCO Publishing, 1985.

Griswold, Terry and D.M. Giangreco. *Delta: America's Elite Counterterrorist Force*. Osceola, WI: MBI Publishing, 1992.

Guerrilla Warfare and Special Forces Operations. Washington, DC: Government Reprints Press, 2001.

Halberstadt, Hans. *U.S. Navy SEALs*. Osceola, WI: Motorbooks International, 1993.

Kelly, Orr. *From a Dark Sky*. New York: Pocket Books, 1997.

Landau, Alan M. and Frieda W. *U.S. Special Forces: Airborne Rangers*. Osceola, WI: MBI Publishing, 1999.

Lanning, Michael Lee. *Inside the LRRPS: Rangers in Vietnam*. New York: Ivy Books, 1988.

Lanning, Michael Lee, and Ray William Stubbe. *Inside Force Recon. Recon Marines in Vietnam*. New York: Ivy Books, 1989.

Leppelman, John. *Blood on the Risers: An Airborne Soldier's Thirty-five Months in Vietnam*. New York: Ivy Books, 1991.

Lewis, Jon E. (Ed.). *True Stories of the Elite Forces*. London: Carroll and Graf, 1993.

Lloyd, Mark. *Special Forces: The Changing Face of Warfare*. London: Arms and Armour Press, 1995.

Lock, John D. *To Fight With Intrepidity: The Complete History of the U.S. Army Rangers, 1622 to Present*. New York: Simon & Schuster, 1998.

Marquis, Susan L. *Unconventional Warfare: Rebuilding U.S. Special Operations Forces*. Washington, DC: Brookings Institution Press, 1997.

McRaven, William H. *Spec Ops: Case Studies in Special Operations Warfare, Theory and Practice*. Novato: Presidio Press, 1998.

Paddock, Alfred H. *U.S. Army Special Warfare: Its Origins*. Lawrence, KS: University Press of Kansas, 2002.

Parker, James E. *Covert Ops: The CIA's Secret War in Laos*. New York: St. Martin's Press, 1995.

Plaster, John L. *SOG: The Secret Wars of America's Commandos in Vietnam*. New York: Onyx, 1998.

Pushies, Fred J. *U.S. Air Force Special Ops*. Osceola, WI: Motorbooks International, 2000.

Pushies, Fred J. *U.S. Army Special Forces*. Osceola, WI: Motorbooks International, 2001.

Ranger Handbook. Fort Benning, GA: Ranger Training Brigade, United States Army Infantry School, 1992.

Special Forces Handbook. Headquarters, Department of the Army, ST31-180.

Special Forces Operational Techniques. Department of the Army Field Manual, FM 31-20.

Tanner, Stephen. *Afghanistan: A Military History from Alexander the Great to the Fall of the Taliban*. New York: Da Capo Press, 2002.

Ste. Croix, Philip de. *Airborne Operations*. London: Salamander Books, 1978.

Tomajczyk, S.F. *US Elite Counter-Terrorist Forces*. Osceola, WI: MBI Publishing Co., 1997.

Walker, Greg. *At the Hurricane's Eye: U.S. Special Operations Forces from Vietnam to Desert Storm*. New York: Ballantine Books, 1994.

Waller, Douglas. *The Commandos*. New York: Simon and Shuster, 1994.

Wimberley, Scott. *Special Forces: Guerrilla Warfare Manual*. Boulder, CO: Paladin Press, 1997.

Zedric, Lance Q., and Michael F. Dilley. *Elite Warriors: 300 Years of America's Best Fighting Troops*. California: Pathfinder Publishing, 1996.

Index